Lincoln Christian College

Given

by the

Lincoln Christian College

Alumni Association

As Part

of a

$100,000 Gift,

1968-1971

D1257343

PROVING GOD

Financial Experiences of the China Inland Mission

PROVING GOD

Financial Experiences of the China Inland Mission

by

PHYLLIS THOMPSON

CHINA INLAND MISSION
Overseas Missionary Fellowship
London, Philadelphia, Toronto, Melbourne, Thun, Cape Town and Singapore

First published 1956
Second edition 1957

Made in Great Britain

Published by the China Inland Mission,
Newington Green, London, N.16,
and printed by The Camelot Press Ltd.,
London and Southampton

Trade Agents: The Lutterworth Press,
4 Bouverie Street, London, E.C.4

266.023
T47

CONTENTS

Allenson 2 75 28 Feb 72

43218

FOREWORD

GOD is utterly trustworthy. His children can have intimate, personal transactions with Him. There is no conceivable situation in which it is not safe to trust Him utterly. Such is the thesis of this book.

For six decades the apostle of faith of the last century, George Muller, conducted five large orphan homes in dependence on God alone, neither making nor permitting any appeal to man. Thousands of orphans were given home and education and brought to the Saviour. But beneficent as was this ministry, he did not conceive it to be the primary object of these institutions. To him they provided a unique opportunity of bringing home to a generation to whom He had become remote, the unfailing faithfulness of God. "The supreme object of these institutions," he wrote, "is *to prove God's faithfulness and the perfect safety of trusting solely to His promises* . . . to lead those who are weak in faith to see that *there is reality in dealing with God alone*."

In the materialistic intellectual climate of our times, when the intervention of God in personal affairs is hardly expected, the message of this book is singularly appropriate and well-timed. Its objective is not to laud a missionary society or to exalt persons who may be incidentally mentioned. Rather does it aim to demonstrate that in our own day and generation God responds magnificently to the trust of His people. Its message is calculated to inspire those who have never been "shut up to God alone" to welcome that experience with a calm, well-founded confidence.

The quarter-century covered in this record, years of

war and revolution on an unprecedented scale, was probably the most disturbed and tumultuous in the ninety years history of the China Inland Mission. Hardly any year of the twenty-five was normal for missionary work. But the very darkness of the background only serves to enhance the wonders of Divine superintendence and deliverance experienced during those days. The deliverance is signal only in proportion as the danger is serious, and is most significant when apart from God we face despair. It would seem as though the sovereign Lord deliberately allowed desperate and impossible situations to arise in order that His servants might have new and unmistakable evidence of His activity on their behalf. Had Lazarus not died, Mary and Martha would not then have realized their Lord as the resurrection and the life—with what tragic impoverishment to themselves and succeeding generations. The very dashing of their hopes and flowing of their tears provided the necessary background for a new revelation of their Master. Divine love permits severe testing, not for its own sake, but because in this crucible alone can faith be purified and strengthened.

To grasp the full significance of this record, the principles upon which the C.I.M. Overseas Missionary Fellowship operates must be understood. Implicit in its constitution is the conviction that we are dealing not with a God who is remote or disinterested, but who always responds to faith and will without fail and in good time meet every need of the worker whom He has called into His harvest-field. Going into debt either as a Mission or as individuals is regarded as being inconsistent with the principle of entire dependence on God. If this is indeed God's work, He is bound to support it. The Mission does not function on the budget system; expenditures are determined by funds received. As to the method of support, "the needs of the work are laid before God in prayer, no person being authorized to solicit funds or take collections on behalf of the Mission." Thus, when the stupendous task of evacuating the 600 missionaries and 200 children scattered over the whole of China was faced, an operation involving the expenditure of £113,000, towards which there was only £1,500 in the Mission treasury, urgent though the need was, no appeal whatever was made. All over the world, however, missionaries and friends laid it before God in prayer. With what result? Not one missionary was detained one day, either in China or on their journey to the homelands, through lack of funds. Every obligation was promptly met.

"He abideth faithful," wrote the founder of the Mission. "If we are really trusting *in Him* and seeking *from Him*, we cannot be put to shame; if not, perhaps the sooner we find the unsoundness of any other foundation the better. The Mission funds or the donors are a poor substitute for the living God."

In this fascinating record we are presented with some striking illustrations of the attributes and activity of our God.

The sovereignty of a God who uses even His enemies to fulfil His beneficent purposes. When all available Mission funds in Communist China had been used and every conceivable source from which money could be imported into the country had dried up, who would have dreamed of the possibility of the Communist Government itself being the unwitting instrument of supplying travel funds for hundreds of missionaries it was expelling from the land? And yet such was the case. Who would have expected urgently needed premises to be provided at a fraction of their cost as the result of a vivid dream which came to a Chinese Buddhist? How safe we can feel when all our affairs are in the hands of a God who is free through friend or foe to work His sovereign will—a will which always moves in the highest interests of His children.

The foreknowledge of a God who is never taken by surprise. In the presence of the famishing multitudes our Lord addressed the question to Philip, "Whence shall we buy bread that these may eat?" This did not imply that He was at a loss to know what to do, for "this He said to prove him, for He Himself knew what He would do," as subsequent events revealed. The apparent impossibility of the situation was quite irrelevant in the presence of the prescient Son of God who always knows what He will do. It is one thing to hold the Divine foreknowledge as an article of belief, but quite a different matter to be the subject of its operation. The greatest degree of human sagacity and foresight could never have anticipated with accuracy the fluctuations of exchange in a world aflame, and made provision accordingly. And yet this has been the experience in the Mission treasury on numerous occasions. Even in the midst of fantastic inflation such as occurred during the Nationalist régime in China, there can be perfect rest of heart with our affairs in the hands of a God who is never taken at a disadvantage.

The accurate timing of a God who is never too late. There are prayers which must be answered by a certain time or not at all. Hundreds of missionaries and two hundred children were to be evacuated to Hongkong, but Mission premises, in that city crowded with refugees, could house only half a dozen, and despite diligent search no further accommodation could be found. How God made the provision in the nick of time is told in these pages, as also what He did just when a pegged exchange was making it absolutely impossible to carry on the work of the Mission. Will not those most vitally concerned be eternally grateful for the opportunity to prove Him as the God who is never too late? It is only by using faith that we are kept from losing it.

The particularity of God's care for His children is writ large on these pages. He does not conduct His work on the assembly-line principle, but evinces an intimate and personal interest in the members of His great family. An elderly missionary, travelling on foot with thousands of other refugees, came to the end of her endurance and was about to fall by the roadside, when strong hands reached down and complete strangers pulled her into an already overcrowded truck. Beleaguered missionaries had for long been without meat. A chicken flew into their isolated compound. A family returning to China found themselves without any money whatsoever as they set out to cross the Pacific. The very day the pooled tips were due an anonymous gift for the exact sum was received. He whose eye is on the sparrow is lovingly concerned with the intimate detail of the daily lives of His children.

The variety of God's method of supply is in keeping with the infinite diversity of His activity in nature. A widow gives a few sacrificial shillings and the gift is multiplied a hundredfold; property is bought in an area where values suddenly increase just prior to its being sold; there is a hitch in a banking procedure; the pressure gauge of an aeroplane goes awry; in no two emergencies does the answer to prayer take the same form. And there is evidence to support the conclusion that the ministry of ravens is not confined to Elijah's day!

But perhaps a miracle greater than any here recorded is that of the phoenix-like resurrection of the Mission after passing through what promised to be conclusive death and burial. What seemed the death-throes of the old proved to be actually the birth-pangs of the new. Six hundred workers sadly emerged from China, but already the field staff of the China Inland Mission

O.M.F. is rapidly nearing the five hundred mark. They work now, not in one country, but in seven, and in twenty-eight languages and dialects. The epic story of the entry of the Overseas Missionary Fellowship into Japan, Formosa, the Philippines, Indonesia, Malaya, Thailand and Indo-China with no experience in tropical lands, no contacts with nationals, and in most cases no languages, will doubtless be told elsewhere, but it has demonstrated anew that the God of Hudson Taylor's day is just the same to-day. The principles on which he founded the work almost a century ago have proved valid in our own day, and these pages, carrying forward as they do the story of faith's quest and conquest, serve to illustrate the continued relevance of those principles in this materialistic age.

J. Oswald Sanders,
Singapore *General Director.*

INTRODUCTION

THE China Inland Mission was formed by James Hudson Taylor in 1865, for the evangelization of the interior of the great Chinese Empire. At that time he was a young married man of thirty-three, home on furlough from China where he had already worked as a missionary for several years. He was connected with no society, and had no wealthy church behind him. It was not until after months of inward uncertainty and conflict that he finally decided to obey what he realized was the Divine urge to found a missionary society of men and women to go to inland China without any guaranteed financial support. On the basis of such promises in God's Word as "Seek ye first the kingdom of God, and His righteousness; and all these things shall be added unto you", he eventually took the step of appealing for consecrated men and women to go with him to the Far East, trusting in God to provide for them. They were engaged in His business, and on Him would they depend for their supplies.

Less than a year after he made his decision, he was on his way back to China with his wife and children, accompanied by sixteen young missionary recruits. The money for their outfits and passages had all come in answer to prayer, and although they did not know where the money for their support in China would come from, they were confident that in some way God would provide. And He did. When funds ran low, more arrived, often from totally unexpected quarters. As with the prophet of old, they proved again and again that the barrel of meal did not waste, neither did the cruse of oil fail.

As the years passed, the Mission grew. The original number of twenty-four members increased to 240, to 480, until at some periods the Mission, with its workers drawn now from America and Australasia as well as Great Britain, and with several Associate societies[1] from countries in Europe, numbered just on 1,400. The number has fluctuated, of course, with the ebb and flow of political power. Membership fell during the devastating Boxer Rebellion in 1900, and rose again. Came the first world war, with the inevitable reduction in missionary recruits. The number rose again. Then came the second world war. After that, as numbers were rising once more, the control of China by the Communists resulted in the withdrawal of all missionary forces from that land.

Now, with the Mission at work in other countries of the Far East, the total membership is rising again, and at present (1957) numbers over 600. Through the ninety years of its history, although no public or private appeal for funds has ever been authorized, its work and workers have been sustained by an unfailing supply. As the number of missionaries, and living costs in the East, have increased, so has its income. When prices have fallen, or the number of workers has been reduced, so have donations diminished. Never has the Mission been in debt when its monthly accounts were balanced. On the other

[1] Associate missions. When the Mission was in China several other societies, mainly from European countries, worked in co-operation with it. These missionary societies supported their own workers, channelling their funds through the Financial Department. While the associate members had their own mission stations, they were included under the title of China Inland Mission, and looked to the leaders at Shanghai for advice and direction in times of perplexity or danger. The number of C.I.M. missionaries listed in China included these members of associate missions. In 1937, for instance, the Mission numbered 1,387, of whom 439 were associate members. Conditions in the new fields in Southeast Asia and Japan did not call for this method of co-operation which proved such a mutual strength in China, and since 1951 the C.I.M. has been composed only of full members, sent from the home centres of North America, Great Britain, Australasia, South Africa and Switzerland.

hand, never has there been so much in hand that money donated could be invested in "gilt-edged securities", even had it been Mission policy to do so!

But such is not the Mission's policy. Funds received are allocated for expenditure during the coming quarter.

When income seems suddenly to be disproportionately high, the reaction of those who must disburse the money is inevitably to ask, "What is this for?" Such a case occurred in 1945. The war in Europe was over, but though the tide had turned in favour of the Allies in the East, victory seemed still in the far distant future. The income of the Mission was normal, meeting all foreseeable needs in the coming quarter, when a gift of £15,000 was unexpectedly received in the London offices.

The Deputy Director of the Mission in China's war-time capital, Chungking, on receiving the news, gasped.

"What is it *for*?" he asked. He was soon to know. The war in the East came to an abrupt and unexpected end with the surrender of the Japanese after the historic dropping of the atomic bombs on Nagasaki and Hiroshima. For four and a half years some hundreds of men, women and children of the C.I.M. had been in captivity. Now the long prayed-for time had come when they could be released, and return to the homelands to receive the nourishment, care and medical attention they would surely require. In addition, the vacant stations in the territory which had been occupied by the Japanese must be opened as soon as possible. It was all going to cost money! It was quite evident now why that extra £15,000 had been sent! "Your Father knoweth what things ye have need of before ye ask."

On the other hand, it would be a distortion of the truth to hide the fact that there have been seasons of extreme straitness. At times the prayer "Give us this day our daily bread" has become an immediate, urgent petition.

Let it be here recorded, however, that if meals have occasionally consisted *mainly* of bread, or its local equivalent, very very rarely have they consisted *only* of bread! At one period during the war, when the cost of living rose to phenomenal heights in China, and an adverse exchange added to the missionaries' financial problems, it was estimated that a slice of bread baked at home cost 3*d.* in Chungking. When economical housekeepers were unable to buy flour, and the bread had to be bought from shops, each slice worked out at 6*d.* Even then, however, there was peanut butter to go on it—a ration of two teaspoonsful a day for each person.

Not only have human beings to be fed and clothed, they have also to be housed. In strange lands, sometimes war-torn, in over-crowded cities where fabulous rents were being demanded and obtained, accommodation has sometimes had to be found at short notice, and with very little money to pay for it. Where, for instance, was the party of eighty-odd missionaries' children and teachers, evacuating from their school in Red China, and due to arrive in two days time in overcrowded Hongkong, to be lodged? The only two C.I.M. families living there were sharing one small flat!

But—— ". . . the birds of the air have nests," said the Son of Man. "Ye are of more value than many sparrows." He who had not where to lay His head but rarely allows His followers to be so placed.

The required accommodation was found in time.

But how? The question arises instinctively to the inquiring mind. Admitted that God has provided all that has been needed to support hundreds of men and women in missionary work in the Far East over a period of some ninety years, what have been the means He has employed? Funds have been forthcoming in answer to prayer, but through what channels have they come?

This book will in some measure answer those questions. It deals mainly with God's provision during the tumultuous quarter of a century through which we have just passed. The full story cannot be related—indeed, only part has been revealed to us. A Master-mind has been behind it all with a foreknowledge and an understanding far beyond our feeble comprehension. In 1949 a party of new recruits was booked to sail from Australia to China, but almost up to the date of sailing only half the passage money was in hand. Just in time a legacy came in which more than met the need. *But the will under which the money had been left was made before any of those young missionaries were born!* A young couple in West China were at the end of their resources. The only money they had in hand was the tithe money they had set apart for the Lord's work, and this they felt they could not use for their own needs. They gave it to the Chinese pastor, who received it with tears in his eyes, saying, "We are just at the end of our rice!" The young missionaries did not tell him they were just at the end of their money, and that their milk bill fell due on the next day! But they had already told their Master. That very evening they received an anonymous gift, sent to them, apparently, from someone on the other side of the world! For in the small things as well as in the great God's intimate love and care has been evident. How came it, for instance, that an English woman missionary who had run right out of tea in a beleaguered city in north China should receive a letter from home *on her birthday*—and in that letter, a little packet of tea! Only One who is of great power, and whose understanding is infinite could have brought the little envelope halfway round a war-torn world, through the gates of a city under the very nose of a Japanese guard to reach a lonely Englishwoman on that day of all others in the year! His mercies are very tender. And His power to provide for

His people, even when they live in the midst of hostility, is as great now as in the days of Elijah. Two of the last four members of the Mission to be released from Communist China were imprisoned in their compound in the far north-west, and unable to obtain permission to draw any money, although their stock of food was now almost exhausted. From no source could they obtain what they needed, and their plight seemed desperate indeed when one day, walking around their yard, they noticed a small roll of corrugated paper lying on the ground. They picked it up, and discovered inside the equivalent of about 30*s.* in Chinese paper money! Where it came from they never knew. They could only assume it had been dropped inadvertently by one of the Communist officials who prowled around on the flat roofs of the Mission buildings. An interesting sidelight on this assumption is the local nickname that was given the black-garbed police by the populace. Because of the colour of their clothes they were dubbed—ravens!

Although the means God uses are not always apparent, however, they are sometimes made quite evident to those who observe these things, and one story of munificent provision made in 1951 has its beginnings as far back as 1885. It is the story of an anonymous gift, received in that year. It has travelled down the years, increasing rather than decreasing in value, and to this day remains intact! It stands out as a thing apart, as though God has chosen it for a special object lesson, rewarding openly what He saw in secret. It is with this story, therefore, that we will commence.

CHAPTER ONE

A PLOT OF LAND

HUDSON TAYLOR was back! He had been away in the humid south for some weeks visiting the little string of mission stations along the Kwangsin River, and within three days was due to set off once more, this time for the distant northern province of Shansi. Tired from his journey as he must have been, there was little opportunity for rest for the founder of the China Inland Mission. A matter of urgent importance had arisen that very day, and a decision must be made before he departed again.

The offer of a plot of land, suitable in position and size for the mission home which was so sorely needed, had just been received. The price asked was £2,500. It was a large sum for those days; more, indeed, than could be afforded for such an object as land for a building. Hudson Taylor was always loath to use money from the General Fund of the Mission for mere property and bricks and mortar! But with the great increase of missionaries coming to the field, the need for a permanent headquarters in Shanghai was becoming urgent. Was this plot of land the beginning of God's answer to the many prayers that had ascended to Him for the provision of a mission home?

Hudson Taylor was not sure, so he called a prayer meeting. To the little company of fellow-workers and missionaries who assembled, he explained the situation. As they knew, the property they were now occupying was rented, and was quite inadequate for the growing missionary family. It would be considerably cheaper in the long run to buy land and build their own premises than to continue renting, besides being much more convenient. Should this suitable but expensive plot of land that was now available be purchased? Was it in God's plan for them to have it? If so, He would certainly supply all that was needed. If it were not, it would be foolhardy indeed to lay out the money. The whole question was one in which Divine guidance was needed, and for that reason the prayer meeting was called.

Now, it happened that at that prayer meeting was a young man named Archibald Orr-Ewing. He had arrived in Shanghai from England eight days previously, and although not yet a member of the C.I.M., he was living in the mission home while learning Chinese. Some years previously he had inherited a fortune of £80,000 from his uncle, and when, at the prayer meeting, he learned of the need of that plot of land, he immediately resolved to buy it. After the prayer meeting he went to Hudson Taylor. He wished to purchase the land in question, and give it as a site for the headquarters of the Mission. The only thing he requested was that his name should be kept out of it.

"The Lord has been dealing with me about not letting people know how He uses His money through me. May I ask you not to tell anyone, unless it is really necessary," he explained simply.

With praise to God and thankfulness to His steward, the offer was accepted. The land was viewed, found suitable in every respect and purchased. The following day Archibald Orr-Ewing set out for the north of China with Hudson Taylor, looking as near a Chinese as a long gown and a pigtail dangling from under a little round black cap would make him. All unknowingly, at the very outset of his missionary career, he had paid for his own memorial!

In view of the size of his fortune and income, that gift

of £2,500 may not appear to be particularly large, or of the same spiritual value as something given as a result of great personal self-denial. Perhaps the spontaneous heartiness with which it was given enhanced its value, for the Scriptures make clear to us the type of giver God loves. Perhaps the self-denial of the whole life of that wealthy young man, who elected to live among Chinese peasants rather than in the comfort of his own spacious Scottish home, added an intrinsic quality to what he gave. Whatever be the reason, that gift has been multiplied through the years, as though taken into the same Hands that received and distributed the five loaves and two small fishes by the Lake of Galilee.

The plot of land in the part of Shanghai known as Hongkew cost £2,500 in 1886. On it were built three large blocks of buildings—also the gift of that same young Scot—which for forty years served as the headquarters of the Mission. When missionary recruits, sometimes fifty at a time, arrived in Shanghai, to that shady, quiet compound they went. During the Boxer Rebellion in 1900, the year of martyrdom when Westerners all over China, in peril of their lives, made their way to the security of the treaty ports, the larger part of the C.I.M. family was lodged there. During the anti-foreign riots of 1927, when a wholesale evacuation of missionaries to the coast became necessary, the buildings on the plot of land at Hongkew again helped to save the situation for the Mission. If rents were extortionate elsewhere in Shanghai, none could be demanded for these premises! After forty years the price paid for them had been saved over and over again.

By 1929, however, it was evident that they were outliving their usefulness. For one thing they were in need of extensive repairs, and for another the Mission had outgrown them. When they were built the C.I.M. comprised some 360 members. Now there were 1,200. Very reluctantly it was decided that if possible larger buildings must be obtained. And, humanly speaking, the hope of obtaining them lay in the plot of ground.

Its value had increased beyond anything young Archibald Orr-Ewing could have foreseen when he bought it. Real estate in Hongkew, Japanese quarter of the great International Settlement, was now at a premium, as its importance as a business and industrial area grew. Mission headquarters, however, had little to gain by being in such an area. A quiet spot where land was cheaper would serve equally well. So the old compound in Hongkew was put in the market, and a piece of ground in the western quarter of the Settlement purchased instead.

That was in 1929. In 1931 a service was held on the new Mission compound in Sinza Road. Two large new blocks of buildings, standing four storeys and six storeys high respectively, were publicly dedicated to the service of God. They were about four times the size of those dilapidated ones just vacated in Hongkew. The buildings themselves, and the major portion of the site on which they stood, had all been paid for by the money received for the plot of land that had originally been bought for £2,500. That £2,500 had been multiplied about thirty-two times!

Were the story to end here, it would be remarkable enough, but it continues. Seven months after the Mission headquarters had been moved from Hongkew to Sinza Road, in the American section, fighting broke out between the Japanese and the Chinese. That such a thing could occur in the apparently unassailable security of the International Settlement was at that time wholly unforeseen—except by God. But the move of C.I.M. headquarters to a district several miles away from the scene of hostilities had been timed with such a Divine precision that even the hard-headed business community in the cosmopolitan port was impressed. The C.I.M. evidently knew when to move! The old premises were right in the thick of the fight, and for the Mission administration to have carried on there would have been out of the question. As it was, in the spacious new buildings, it was a case of business as usual!

Not that C.I.M. headquarters were always preserved from the perils of war. Indeed, from 1943 to 1945, they actually became the Shanghai Defence headquarters of the invading Japanese! This proved, however, to be a greater advantage than was at first recognized. A great deal of wanton damage was inflicted on many buildings in Japanese occupied cities, but naturally enough, those with high-ranking officers in residence were better preserved. When the war was over, and missionaries returned to view the property, this was the report:

> The two large blocks of buildings are structurally sound, and have suffered little wanton damage, though boilers and radiators and a good deal of furniture and equipment were removed. But we are far more amazed at the quantity and relatively good condition of what remains to us than by what we have lost.

It seemed then that peace had come to stay, and that missionary work could be resumed throughout China for a prolonged period. But it was not to be. The Communist forces in the north overran the whole country with a rapidity greater than had been thought possible. In the early days of their political supremacy it was hoped it would be possible for missionaries to remain and work in China. By the summer of 1950, however, it was becoming evident how difficult that was going to be and by the end of the year even C.I.M. decided it was impossible. In December the decision was made to withdraw its missionaries from China.

It was the saddest hour in the history of the Mission. There had been more tragic ones as, for instance, the Boxer Rebellion of 1900, when fifty-eight missionaries and twenty-one of their children had been cruelly murdered. But none more sad than this. From large and small stations, in populous cities and isolated border towns, little groups of missionaries started to move towards the coast, drawing out of China. They were leaving, so far as they could tell, never to return. For eighty-six years, through war and civil strife, anti-foreign uprisings and Japanese occupation, the Mission had remained on in the land. To leave it now, to say farewell to Chinese fellow-believers who must stay on under a régime which bases its whole policy on the assumption that "There is no God", was heart-rending.

But the situation had to be faced. The presence of Western missionaries, so far from easing the situation for the Chinese Christians, merely seemed to make matters worse. The sooner they could depart, the more likelihood there appeared to be of churches being allowed to carry on without interference. Furthermore, the property of missionary societies all over China was liable to be taken over by the People's Government at any time. Some had already gone, and news was constantly being received of this or that mission compound being occupied by Communist officials or employees. As far as the C.I.M. was concerned, its work being mainly evangelistic, it owned comparatively few valuable premises beyond five or six hospitals. Many church buildings had already been handed over years previously to the local church councils. There was, however, one property which was of considerable value, and of vital importance to the Mission at this time of emergency. That property was, of course, the headquarters in Sinza Road.

If only this could be retained until the withdrawal of the

hundreds of missionaries and their children was well under way! It was just the sort of place that would appeal to a bureaucratic government department. The prospect of being evicted from these buildings that had always in a singular way seemed a loving gift from God, to make room for those who openly disbelieved in His very existence was an unwelcome one indeed. For His own Name's sake, prayer was constantly made that this might not happen.

And God answered prayer. That original gift, given over sixty years previously, was still in His Hands. Until He chose to relinquish it, none could pluck it thence. In a new way, now, it was to be used for the succour of His servants.

One day, early in 1951, when financial problems of evacuating hundreds of people from a country whose Government was eager to be rid of them, yet strangely loath to let them go, were large and varied, news was received that a hospital committee was on the look-out for premises, and that those in Sinza Road seemed eminently suitable for their requirements. Cautious inquiries were set on foot. The result seemed too good to be true. The hospital, connected with a military commission, wished to rent the larger block of buildings, and was prepared to pay three years' rent in advance, and sign an agreement to that effect!

The Directors of the Mission had little expectation of receiving the money, but welcomed the prospect of the beloved buildings being used as a hospital rather than as government offices. Not only would this arrangement seem more in accordance with the purpose for which they had been erected, but would also ensure that they would not be requisitioned out of hand in the immediate future, when they were still so greatly needed by the Mission. After a certain amount of discussion, inspection of property, etc., a rental agreement was therefore drawn up whereby, on an agreed date, the larger block should be taken over by the hospital authorities, on certain conditions.

To the uninitiated it might well seem that it merely remained for the agreement to be signed and the affair would be settled. In actual fact, however, the drawing up of an agreement acceptable to both parties was but the beginning of the matter. Not so easily could Westerners manage their affairs under the People's Government. Before the agreement could be signed, permission must be obtained from the Foreign Affairs Bureau.

The Foreign Affairs Bureau loomed large on the horizon of every foreigner in China. It was the Foreign Affairs Bureau to which they must apply for permission to leave the country. It was from the Foreign Affairs Bureau they must obtain a permit to travel, and to which they must report when they did so. If they imagined they could sell their goods, or even give them away as they chose, they soon discovered that they were mistaken. The Foreign Affairs Bureau had a say in the matter. The say was usually "No." In fact, foreigners soon stopped applying for permission. They just gave up the idea that they could do what they liked with their own.

When the agreement was duly drawn up, therefore, it had first to be presented to the F.A.B. (Foreign Affairs Bureau). After very earnest prayer it was submitted with a note to the effect that the agreement would be signed on the following day—unless the F.A.B. forbad them to do so.

The F.A.B. of course, promptly refused to give permission.

Now there is a subtle difference between refusing to give permission, and actually forbidding an action. The F.A.B. for once was in somewhat of a quandary. The automatic reaction to any suggestion of a foreigner from one of the "imperialist" nations that he be allowed to sell or rent any of his property met a distinct check in this case. The F.A.B. could not help realizing that by forbidding the signing of the agreement, they were forbidding not only a foreign missionary society, but a hospital under the authority of the highest military commission in East China. There is something about high military commissions that makes even People's Government Bureaux reluctant to oppose them, it seems! So the C.I.M. was not forbidden to sign the agreement, it was merely not given permission to do so. And after some parleying, the F.A.B. said that *if* it were signed, a copy of the contract was to be sent to them.

It was a step forward, and at C.I.M. headquarters that night there was rejoicing—with trembling. The following day the agreement was signed, and a copy duly sent to the F.A.B.

Tr-ing! Tr-ing! The telephone bell rang. The F.A.B. was at the other end of the line, and commanded that no payments were to be received from the hospital until the Bureau had ratified the agreement.

The Bureau did not ratify the agreement.

In some ways it was not a great disappointment, for in view of what was happening to others, it had seemed too much to expect that this matter would go through. But the desire for the buildings to be used as a hospital rather than for other purposes, was great. As the days passed and no word was heard from the F.A.B. those at Sinza Road continued in prayer, and tentative inquiries were made as to the fate of the agreement. Then, after three weeks, the F.A.B. broke their silence.

They were not encouraging. The agreement could not in any circumstances go through as it stood, they said. Six changes must be made in it before it could be ratified.

Those dealing with the matter for the C.I.M. had little doubt where the trouble lay. It had to do with the payment of three years' rent in advance, of course, and other matters of like importance. To assume that they could actually obtain rent money, and retain the title deeds of the property had been expecting too much, and might well be landing them into difficulties now. The situation looked serious, but it had to be faced, so those responsible went to face it.

The F.A.B officials were extremely annoyed. The agreement was drawn up in a way that was an affront to the People's Government of China. And those representing the Mission, knowing how easy it was to affront that sensitive body, meekly affirmed that no affront had been intended, and requested to know how it had unwittingly been offered.

When they heard, they could scarcely believe it. The affront had nothing to do with the rent. It had nothing to do even with its being paid in advance. Nor was it concerning the retention of the title deeds. The affront, to put it baldly, had to do with—the drains!

In the agreement was a simple clause, usually included in such documents, requiring that those renting the property should keep the plumbing in good working order. This clause, it was asserted, was derogatory to the People's Government of China. If it is a little obscure as to whether the insult lay in the suggestion that the People's Government might fail to keep the drains in order, or in mentioning them at all, it does not greatly matter. The Mission was quite willing to delete this clause, and others equally unimportant. When this was done, the agreement was rewritten, signed, sealed and delivered. And what perhaps was most surprising of all, a large deposit was paid into the Mission bank account! In all, *three years' rent in advance was received for this building.*

Nor was that all. At that time foreign organizations were being forbidden to sell anything, but the F.A.B. actually granted the C.I.M. permission to dispose of a considerable amount of equipment and furniture to the hospital—which was also paid for! Then, as missionaries were steadily withdrawing, and the main administrative work was being done in Hongkong rather than in Shanghai, it was evident that the rest of the Sinza Road property would soon be vacated. Negotiations were set on foot to rent the second large block to the hospital, the agreement was duly signed, and six months' rent was paid in advance.

Probably only those who were in China at that time can appreciate how remarkable a thing it was that all this should happen. On all sides foreign premises were being taken over, on some pretext or other, without being paid for. For the C.I.M. property and equipment on Sinza Road, however, the sum of J.M.P.[1] 1,000,000,000 was received, equivalent to approximately £28,570!

Just what this money meant to a Mission with about 800 men, women and children to bring from all parts of China down to Hongkong it is difficult to express. The money could not be taken out of the country. There was no other way in which it could be used but in personal expenses. It was just provided, it seemed, to see the Mission out of China. It proved sufficient to pay all the exorbitant demands made for "severance pay" of servants and employees of the Mission throughout the land, and to provide travelling expenses of almost the entire Mission down to Hongkong without stint or need for economy. Never, probably, had C.I.M. missionaries been so free to travel by plane, or to book first-class sleepers on trains if they were in the regions where such luxuries were available! There was plenty of money to pay for them!

[1] J.M.P. Chinese abbreviation for "People's currency".

And the crowning marvel is that the Sinza Road property still belongs to the C.I.M.! Nothing else in China does. All the other property went. But the Mission still holds the title deeds of those two great buildings and the land on which they stand. Is it a symbol of a tree that has been hewn down but whose root remains in the earth—a root that may yet shoot forth branches again? Be that as it may, one thing is sure. The story of that compound will always be connected with the story of a young man in the clothes of a Chinese peasant, who refused to allow his name to be known as the donor of gifts running into thousands of pounds, and who wrote from a lonely inland city:

"I do thoroughly believe that to be a really useful and faithful steward . . . one must deny oneself. . . ." All through his life he was frugal in the matter of personal expenditure. On one occasion he signed a contract for the building of large premises to be given to the Mission at the close of a day when he had tramped for twenty miles over rough dusty roads in inland China. As an elderly man at home in Britain, he caused some anxiety to his family by refusing to travel by taxi unless by doing so he could give a lift to someone else! Quite simply and practically he followed the example of his Master who, though He was rich, yet for our sakes became poor, that we, through His poverty, might be rich.

CHAPTER TWO

HELD BY THE ENEMY

"THE Haymans, Bosshardts and Miss Emblen have been taken captive by the Reds."

"The Stams have been captured by the Reds."

"*The Stams have been murdered. . . .*"

The last three months of 1934 were solemn ones as news of captivity and martyrdom reached the headquarters of the C.I.M. The army, later known as the Eighth Route, in which Mao Tze-tung and Chu Teh were among the leaders, was passing through the provinces south of the Yangtze, leaving desolation and despair in its train. Towns and villages were pillaged, men, women, and even children dragged to captivity and death, as the Communist rebels marched grimly over the mountains and plains in search of a region in which they could gain complete control. It was not until a year or two later that the Nationalist Government troops in the south finally proved too strong for them and they struck northwards to establish themselves in their stronghold in Yenan—biding their time for nearly fifteen years until they eventually gained control of the whole country.

If the martyrdom of John and Betty Stam, the long captivity of Arnolis Hayman and the even longer one of Alfred Bosshardt were among the subtly-planned thrusts of the devil at the work of God, they have merely served to prove once more that in all things we are conquerors through Him that loved us. Suffering and sacrifice, after all, have proved even more fruitful than service. There are too many men and women on the mission-field to-day who were first turned towards it because of those who sealed their testimony with their blood, to be able to doubt that. While it is easy to see these things in retrospect however, hearts made tender by love cannot but yearn over those on whose heads the storm is breaking. And whose heart is more tender than that of the Father who knoweth our frame, remembering we are but dust?

The story of John and Betty Stam is too well known to need repeating here, nor is this book concerned so much with the invisible supplies of grace and courage God gives to the spirit, as with the tangible and visible provision He makes for the body. And in this particular case, with a very tiny body—a three-months-old, blue-eyed baby girl; Helen Priscilla Stam.

She had been carried in her father's arms, captive as he was, from Tsingteh to a neighbouring town. She had spent the night in her mother's arms, in the same dark room in which her father was tightly bound to the post of the heavy bed. Early the next morning she was left alone, as her young parents, stripped of their outer clothes, hands bound behind them, were led out to die. For thirty hours she lay there, alone. And when eventually she was picked up, it was by a Chinese evangelist, himself a penniless refugee with a wife and a sick child. It was 100 miles over the mountains to the nearest missionaries, through bandit-infested country, and the evangelist was a timid man. Besides, he had his own sick child to consider. He might well have shirked the journey. But those invisible supplies of grace and courage were being poured into his heart, as though from the overflow granted to the young missionary couple who had with such amazing calmness just laid down their lives. He picked up the little white baby and carried her to his wife to care for while he went to look for the bodies of her parents. And when he had found them and made arrangements for their burial, and preached to the crowd of people that had gathered, he prepared to set out, with his wife and a man to carry his own sick child and little Helen Priscilla Stam in two baskets on a pole slung across his shoulders, to walk that 100 miles to the nearest mission station.

And this is where the visible and tangible provision for the body comes into the story. The evangelist had been robbed of all his money. So, indeed, had nearly everyone else. "Famine relief money and our personal money and effects are all in their hands," wrote John Stam in the brief letter he was able to smuggle into the post the day before he died. But when the evangelist's wife gently drew little Helen out of her sleeping bag, she found tucked away inside it a clean nightdress, some clean diapers, and *two five dollar bills carefully pinned to them*!

How Betty Stam had been able to retain those ten dollars is a mystery, but there they were, her last provision, with that tiny bundle of clean clothes, for her little daughter! And it was just sufficient. The ten dollars provided for the little party that set off on that 100-mile journey over the mountains. The evangelist's wife was even able to purchase a tin of baby's food with which to feed the tiny white girl in her care. And when the missionary into whose arms the little bundle was placed looked into it, he saw the plump, healthy face of his martyred friends' child, peacefully sleeping. How perfectly had the Eternal Father known the needs of that tiny frame!

He knew, too, the needs of the frames of the two men who were being dragged through weary days of ceaseless travel by another section of the same Red Army that was responsible for the execution of the Stams. It was in October, 1934, that Mr. and Mrs. Bosshardt, Mr. and Mrs. Hayman and Miss Grace Emblen were taken captive in Kweichow. The two wives were released almost immediately, and Miss Emblen after a few days, but Mr. Hayman was held captive for nearly a year, while it was eighteen months before Mr. Bosshardt was released. Sometimes it was only after a forced march lasting two days and a night that they were able to lie down to rest. Had it not been for the quiet, almost imperceptible supplies of just what was needed, sometimes in the most unexpected places and through the most unlikely channels, the two Westerners could scarcely have survived. There is an ironical humour in the fact that often enough those supplies came, quite unwittingly, through the Communists themselves! Imagine the captives' surprise and delight (carefully concealed) for instance, when they became the possessors of some tins of Carnation milk and tinned tomatoes at a place where their captors stopped for a few days! The Chinese did not know their use—they preferred fat pork, if they could obtain it! Nor did they think much of the large Swiss cheese which they had obtained somewhere! "It is an acquired taste," agreed their prisoner—and then, hoping against hope, he intimated that it was a taste he had acquired! He was imprisoned in a sort of cage, built inside the yamen, at the time. Perhaps it is necessary to be similarly situated to realize just what the addition to his prison fare of the few sections of that cheese which were pushed through the bars meant to him. Such tangible evidences of the invisible Father's compassion bring Him very near.

At the very outset of the long and painful period of captivity they had such an evidence; a gentle tempering of the storm that broke around them. When Mr. and Mrs. Bosshardt were captured on the road, all their belongings were taken from them. That was not surprising. But in quite a short time they were returned! The Communist who was acting as judge commanded it. Furthermore, he asked them if they had received everything back, and when Mr. Bosshardt looked through them, and said he could not find his travelling money, he demanded,

"How much did you have?"

"Twelve dollars," replied Alfred Bosshardt.

"Give them twelve dollars," said the judge. And twelve dollars were handed over. It was not until some time later that the missionaries discovered their own twelve dollars were safely tucked inside their bedding rolls! Mr. and Mrs. Hayman with their two small children, and Miss Emblen had been taken by this time. They were all to be held for ransom. $100,000 was to be demanded for each one. Captives as they were now, knowing full well that such sums could never be paid for their deliverance, their immediate and urgent need was for a little ready cash! Unhappy indeed was the prisoner who must rely entirely on the generosity of guards. But the Haymans and Miss Emblen had been allowed no opportunity to bring anything with them, and when they faced the unknown future, with the prospect of joining the company of weary captives who had perforce to follow the rebel army over the mountain paths, they would have been empty-handed had it not been for those twenty-four silver dollars.

What that sum of money, comparatively small as it was, meant to the prisoners, it is impossible to estimate. During the first month of their captivity the two men were marched almost ceaselessly in those forced stages—a day, a night and a day—before they could rest. The food given them was of the coarsest, and weary as they became, they could scarcely digest it. Had it not been for the better food they were occasionally able to buy with the money which had been so remarkably provided, it is doubtful whether they could have survived the sudden strain of those first bitter weeks. There were plenty who could not stand the strain, and therefore did not survive. Prisoners who could not keep up in the march were just left behind—dead. But although Arnolis Hayman was a man no longer young, and Alfred Bosshardt was dragged for eighteen months in the wake of the ruthless army, they both came out alive. The Father's provision for His captives had not failed.

That same provision, with all its foreknowledge and preparation, was revealed in the far greater captivity of the war in the Far East.

It was on December 7th, 1941, that the Japanese made their sudden, unexpected attack on Pearl Harbour, thus openly taking their place in the conflict that was raging between the Allies and the Axis powers. A few hours later two gun-boats on the Yangtze were attacked. The American boat, taken by surprise, surrendered. The English *Petrel* went down fighting against impossible odds. Japan was at war with the U.S.A. and Britain.

There were 250 members of the C.I.M. in that part of China which was occupied by the Japanese. In addition there were over 200 C.I.M. children of missionaries in the Chefoo schools. They were all virtually captives from that day. And, of course, they were cut off from their sources of supply in the home countries. It was nearly a year, however, before they were concentrated in internment camps, during which time they had to be supplied with money. And in spite of the impossibility of doing it, they all *were* supplied with money. God's material provision did not cease with the freezing of foreign funds, or the confiscation of foreign property. But how did He do it? What were the means He used?

In the first place, it is a rather surprising fact that during the year 1941 the Mission's income had shown a considerable increase. In view of the horrors of the blitz, with its destruction of life, limb and property, donations from hard-pressed, heavily-taxed Britain might well have fallen off. In the first year of the war, they did, but after that they started to rise again. And it is interesting to observe that in 1939, when contributions from Great Britain to China fell by about £4,000, they rose in North America by some £9,000! Furthermore, during the years 1940 and 1941, there had been a considerable gain on exchange, as the accompanying table indicates.

Received in China from	*1941*			*1940*			*1939*			*1938*		
	£	*s.*	*d.*	£	*s.*	*d.*	£	*s.*	*d.*	£	*s.*	*d.*
Gt. Britain	35,275	1	10	22,839	5	3	21,755	13	4	25,865	13	6
N. America	28,418	0	10	23,761	19	4	29,455	19	3	20,041	18	6
Australasia	1,991	16	6	3,684	1	3	3,220	11	6	3,126	11	3
China	3,901	11	2	3,042	4	4	3,880	3	6	4,393	12	9
Bank interest	103	18	10	266	8	6	85	4	5	3,171	10	3
Gain in exchange ..	3,932	9	2	3,946	18	4						
	£73,622	18	4	£57,540	17	0	£58,397	12	0	£56,599	6	3

But most marked is the increase in the Mission's income on the field during 1941. Here we see it to be £16,000 more than in the previous year. At the time when the tide of war seemed flowing steadily against the Allies, when tension was increasing in the Far East, while Rommel and his Afrika Korps were winning their spectacular victories in North Africa, Mission headquarters in Great Britain was able to send over one-third more than in the previous year—an increase of over £12,000!

That suddenly increased income was the Heavenly Father's quiet, unostentatious provision against the lean years that lay ahead. The possibility of war breaking out in the Far East was foreseen by the Mission leaders, but they could have done little to prepare for the emergency had it not been for that added income. As it was, for the whole year missionaries received a remittance slightly above normal, enabling them to enter the long period of emergency in Free China, and captivity in the Japanese-occupied zone, with durable clothing and well-stocked larders! And although in the years to come the clothing became threadbare and patched, and the cupboard often looked as bare as that of the proverbial Mrs. Hubbard, that early bounteous provision in a wonderful way helped to "break the fall".

But that was not all of God's provision, nor would it, in itself, have been sufficient. Two hundred and fifty men and women and 200 children had to be supported for a year in enemy-occupied territory, and then supplied with food parcels for a further period, in most cases, of nearly three years. Had this long period been foreseen, it would have seemed an impossible situation. But God knew, and He prepared in good time. As is so often the case, His most important preparation was—men.

One of those men was Frank Parry. He was the child of C.I.M. missionaries, and had early pledged his own allegiance to his father's God. "Lord, what wilt Thou have *me* to do?" was his prayer when, as a young bank clerk, he returned to his lodgings in London each evening and knelt by his bed for the quarter of an hour he set aside daily to seek his Master's will for his life. Guidance was not denied. Quite clearly it was indicated—China and the C.I.M. But before he set sail for the land he already knew and loved, at the suggestion of the General Director, he received special training with a view to helping in the financial department in Shanghai, if needed. He little knew that one of the most critical periods in the Mission's history, 1941, would find him in charge of it!

He was not alone. Two younger men, with all the daring readiness to take risks that characterizes youth, were with him. And when, on December 9th, 1941, the Japanese took over control in Shanghai, it devolved on the men in the financial department of C.I.M. to prepare for what proved to be a long financial siege.

This is how they did it. It had always been the policy of C.I.M. to convert money from abroad into Chinese currency, so this crisis found them with plenty of cash in hand. In fact, they had too much! The accounts at Shanghai covered the whole field, and the money that would normally have been expended within a few months was now tied up for the duration of war. Chinese currency was already in the momentum of rapid inflation, and accounts that looked quite substantial now would soon be worthless. The enterprising men in the financial department prayed for guidance and looked for a way.

It was not long before they discovered that if C.I.M. was almost embarrassed by its large stock of Chinese money, there were other missionaries and Christian organizations in Shanghai who were even more embarrassed by their lack of it! Sterling and U.S.$ they had in plenty, but it was Chinese dollars they needed to buy their daily bread and pay their outstanding accounts. All the official exchanges were closed now, of course, and for many of God's servants in those days C.I.M. proved to be the one place where they could obtain Chinese money. Without that unofficial exchange they would have been in difficult straits indeed. And those transactions proved to be of mutual benefit. The big sums of Chinese money which C.I.M. held were being converted into currencies that would retain their value. Mission finance was conserved by this means.

Then there was the run on American and British banks. They were closing down. The Japanese cut all balances in half, and then ordained that half of what remained must be left in a "blocked" account. The remainder, however, could be drawn out, providing there was someone to apply for it in person. Long queues of people waiting to draw their money formed outside the banks, and in those queues were members of the C.I.M. headquarters staff. Some of them went day after day, carrying a different bank book each time! Missionaries' private banking accounts were kept in Shanghai, and Frank Parry had obtained permission from members of the Mission all over China to draw out their private money. Few of them amounted to a great deal, it is true, but the accumulated sum total was a very welcome, and not inconsiderable addition, to the exchequer.

Now came the question of what to do with the cash that was being obtained. American and British currencies, however they might retain their value on the international exchange, were not easily negotiable in Japanese-occupied Shanghai. To lay in a store of Chinese or Japanese paper money, however, liable to daily depreciation as it was, was obviously useless. There was just one form of currency which was always negotiable, and whose value did not change—and that was GOLD. More to be desired than any other currency at this time, was gold—if it could be obtained.

In the months before internment, therefore, the men in the financial department started buying gold. It had to be done with the utmost secrecy. They took some of those quiet little journeys of theirs to obtain it at the risk of their lives, and they knew it. Harrowing stories of the tortures inflicted on Chinese caught trading outside the Japanese monopoly ring did not fail to reach their ears. But it was their responsibility to make what provision was possible for the missionaries and children whose finances were in their hands. "We ought to lay down our lives for the brethren," says the Scripture. Of course! They were prepared to do it. So off they went on those secret little errands to Chinese merchants, any one of whom might have betrayed them—but none did! Time and time again they returned to the large Sinza Road headquarters with tiny little packets which were slipped into a hiding place behind an innocent-looking bookcase. Gold does not require much space!

But the days of even restricted liberty were ebbing out. Internment camps were being prepared, and it was evident that all Westerners belonging to the Allied nations would soon be in them. Money in "safe currencies" or gold bars would be equally useless then! But what man could not have prepared for was already foreseen by the One who knows the end from the beginning. That money, so wisely collected, was for a purpose—to sustain life. Sustain life it did. For God had again made His provision—of men who would stand in a gap.

Some months before the outbreak of war between the Allies and Japan, a group of German C.I.M. associate missionaries working in inland China were deported by the Chinese authorities to Hongkong. From there they made their way up to Shanghai where they were, of course, gladly received into the C.I.M. headquarters. Their help in the financial department and mission home was welcomed, and when eventually war broke out and the Japanese police officials marched in to assert their authority, they were not a little taken aback to discover that among this body of American and British missionaries there were also several Germans, and that apparently they were all living harmoniously together!

The German missionaries, of course, were in quite a different category from the others. No internment camp for them! They were courteously invited to take up residence in a smaller compound in another part of Shanghai. As members of one of the Axis powers, they were treated with respect. Obligingly, they departed to the new home allotted to them, taking their belongings with them—together with the Mission account books, a large supply of money in sterling and U.S. dollars, and the gold bars! And for the next two or three years the task that took priority over all others for some of them was that of scouring Shanghai for the most nourishing, tasty, yet inexpensive food they could buy; packing it into separate cartons, one for each interned C.I.M. missionary in the Shanghai area; and sending them monthly into the internment camps! Month after month, without fail, those food parcels were sent in. With what earnest prayers, with what care and love, were they prepared and packed! Not without some trepidation and the exercise of extreme caution were they conveyed, in small and inconspicuous consignments, to the Red Cross Headquarters. Shanghai was under martial law, with guards on the streets, and people showing interest in the occupants of internment camps were viewed with suspicion. But the risk was always taken. The German fellow-workers and faithful Chinese friends provided a life-line that never failed. Life-line indeed it was.

"I think it would be true to say that but for the extra nourishment we in the Shanghai area received through the parcels sent in, some of us would not have survived the ordeal. We owe our lives to the overruling providence of God in sending that small group of German associate missionaries to Shanghai just before Pearl Harbour, and enabling them to minister to us in our time of need." So wrote one who knew from personal experience what those food parcels meant. "We owe them a big debt of gratitude for their unremitting labour and the risks they took on our behalf. All the other groups of German missionaries were placed under surveillance or interned up country and so needed assistance; only this one group came through to Shanghai, and was well established there before we became enemy nationals to the Japanese." The deportation had all been part of God's planning, after all!

The war ended at last. The internees were released. The high ranking Japanese officers vacated the premises in Sinza Road, and missionaries again took possession. One of the first things those in Emergency headquarters in Chungking did when peace was declared was to make arrangements for funds to be sent to Shanghai by air, for the released internees. "We were purposely most generous in the amount sent, so as to relieve our friends of any possible feeling of financial stringency." If there was to be any stringency those in Emergency headquarters were prepared to bear the brunt of it. But there was none. When the task of taking over the accounts and clearing up all the financial arrangements made in Shanghai was completed, this was the report:

> The total assets were found to provide a generous reconstruction of all balances, the wherewithal to meet every bill and commitment during the internment years, including food parcels, and finally to make a considerable grant to all internees for re-equipment. Praise the Lord, it is wonderful to be able to do all this!

The story of the "safe currencies" and the gold bars is nearly finished now. How different would have been the financial report at the end of the war had they never been obtained! How much money would have been lost had the accounts been allowed to remain in Chinese currency! For the gold bars that had cost 125,000 Chinese dollars in 1942, were now worth 33 million!

CHAPTER THREE

THE FLEDGLINGS

THE charge is not infrequently levelled at missionaries that a great deal of unjust suffering and privation is inflicted on their children. That most of them must endure an early separation from their parents is undeniable, and who would desire to underestimate the sacrifice this involves? Few would, however, deny that the greater suffering is borne by the parents. To many a labourer on the mission field to-day the sword has pierced deepest and keenest at the words "He that loveth . . . son or daughter more than Me is not worthy of Me." Nevertheless, there are few parents of the C.I.M. who have not proved that the Hand that holds the sword also applies the balm. The God they serve is not as Molech, to whom his worshippers must pass their children through the fire. And as far as C.I.M. is concerned, the balm He applied for nearly sixty years was—Chefoo.

It was in 1879 that Hudson Taylor went to that bracing, healthy seaside town in north China. It was one of the occasions when he seemed near to death's door, but the fresh sea breezes after the humidity of inland cities did wonders for him; and as he recovered health, an idea formulated in his mind. Were there not fellow-workers inland needing just such rest and life-restoring air as he was having? And were there not little children, needing an education beyond that which their busy missionary parents could supply? What better place for both school and holiday-home than this very spot? So he bought a plot of land. It was a bean-field, actually, with a gully and fresh water running down beside it. And as the exchange happened to be very much in his favour at the time, it cost remarkably little.

On the plot of land was built a house—five rooms upstairs and five rooms down, with a few lean-to rooms besides. The timber was largely obtained from old ships that had been wrecked in the bay. And there were started the Chefoo Schools for the children of C.I.M. missionaries. Two small boys were the first scholars, but others were soon added to their number. For over fifty years the children of missionaries, instead of being sent home, went to Chefoo on the healthy north China coast, there to obtain an education equivalent to that of a public school in England. To Chefoo went their parents when holidays became due. From Chefoo went the children whose parents lived in accessible places, to spend their Christmas holidays at home! Balm indeed to parents whose hearts felt lacerated at the necessary separation from their children was the very name of Chefoo.

And that the school was a gift direct from the Hand of God is evidenced by the fact that practically the whole cost of the large buildings which eventually had to be erected was met by gifts specially donated for the purpose. They were not paid for out of Mission funds. When it was realized that a new building for the Boys' School would cost £5,000, for instance, with what joy was a letter received in which were the words,

> The Lord has laid it on my heart to bear the entire cost of building the new school.

"The Lord has laid it on my heart. . . ." Could any doubt from whose Hand came the balm?

Not only did the Chefoo schools provide an easing balm for parents' hearts, however. They proved an active and effective agency for the extension of the Kingdom of God.

To assess their full spiritual results is, of course, impossible. Many members of other missions, and business people in the East, sent their children there, and it has been out of the question to follow up all who decided to follow Christ while in the schools. Nor has any sort of statistical table of the Preparatory School been prepared. A number of children attended that who for one reason or another did not go on to the Senior Schools. It has, however, been possible to obtain some approximate statistics concerning those who passed through the two Senior Schools into full-time missionary work.

Some 2,116 boys and girls passed through the Chefoo Schools, of whom 756 were the children of C.I.M. missionaries, to meet whose needs the schools were run. It is with these children that the statistics deal.

The total number of boys who passed through the Boys' School was 1,190. Of these, 414 were C.I.M. children. Of those 414 boys

34 joined the C.I.M. =8·2%
23 joined other missions=5·5%=13·7%

The total number of girls who passed through the Girls' School was 926. Of these, 342 were C.I.M. children. Of these 342 girls

77 joined the C.I.M. =22·5%
18 joined other missions=5·3%=27·8%

Many others, of course, have served the Lord in various ways in the homelands, but these statistics deal entirely with those who went to serve God on the foreign mission field; twenty out of every hundred, or an average of nearly three for every year since the School was started in a house built largely of the timber from wrecked ships, with two small boys as the first scholars, to the day in 1942 when they all had to leave the beloved compound for internment camp.

The school was never to be re-opened in Chefoo, although none realized it then. But as the boys marched out of the gates, carrying suitcases and satchels, footballs and cricket bats, unprompted by the masters they suddenly burst into song.

> God is still on the throne,

they sang, young chins in the air and shoulders squared,

> And He will remember His own,
> Tho' trials may press us, and burdens distress us,
> He never will leave us alone.
> God is still on the throne,
> And He will remember His own,
> His promise is true, He will not forget you,
> God is still on the throne.

So, past the astonished Japanese guards they marched into captivity.

The school buildings were left behind—but not so easily were they separated from their goodly heritage.

That God's compassions where the children are concerned did not cease with the closing of the schools in Chefoo has been shown in many ways since then. One little story from those war years in China illustrates with peculiar significance His foreknowledge and care for the little fledglings who, for His sake, have so early been thrust from their own nests. The story has to do with an extra load of petrol on an aeroplane.

It was late in 1944, when the Japanese were pressing towards Chungking. Instructions were received that the little kindergarten school in Kiating which had been opened for the children of C.I.M. missionaries in Free China was to be evacuated to India. An American army lorry arrived at the Mission compound to collect the twenty-five children and two missionaries who were to accompany them, and convey them to the airfield. They spent Christmas Day there, waiting for the plane that was to take them to Kunming and thence across the mountains of Indo-China and Burma to India. Hearty helpings of turkey and Christmas pudding served on metal trays by generous G.I.'s did much to maintain tradition, while adding zest to the occasion, and the festivity usually connected with the season was by no means lacking, in spite of the unusual circumstances! It was not until late afternoon that the plane actually arrived and the children, hugging dolls, toy trains or stamp albums clambered excitedly up the gangway for their first aeroplane trip.

"We haven't got parachutes for children, so we can't give them any," observed a member of the crew to one of the women, as they watched the little ones scrambling into their seats. "You wouldn't jump without the children, so it's no use giving them to you. And we wouldn't jump without you—so I guess we just won't take any parachutes this trip."

They got settled at last. The door was shut. The engine started to hum. Then, suddenly, it was switched off. Something was wrong with the pressure gauge, they heard the pilot say. It must be repaired before they could start. And then he added casually, "Might as well load on some more petrol while we're waiting." No, he knew they didn't need it, but they might as well load it now—it would save time when preparing for the next trip.

The pressure gauge was repaired, the petrol loaded, and eventually the plane took off as darkness was falling. It usually took about two hours to reach Kunming, but two hours found them still flying high.

"When do we reach Kunming?" one of the missionaries asked a member of the crew.

"Oh, in about an hour or so," he replied vaguely.

What he did not tell her was that an air raid warning in Kunming had resulted in a black-out and that the pilot had lost his bearings. They were flying around in the dark, over unknown, mountainous territory, afraid to come down low because of the hills, unable to distinguish any familiar landmark. And, of course, the petrol was running out.

They flew on and on. Oxygen was handed round, but soon that was all used up, and some of the children got sick, gasping for breath. Still the pilot could not get his bearings. The petrol tank would run dry in another half an hour and then. . . .

But there were twinkling lights suddenly discerned below. The pilot, straining his eyes, recognized them. They were over an airfield! Not of Kunming, to be sure, but an airfield. A place to land, free of mountain peaks or paddy-fields, at last! Down, down came the plane, piloted with immeasurable relief to the flat surface of levelled ground.

"Let me get out and kiss terra firma!" ejaculated one of the crew as he came out from the crew cabin. "Never again!" For he knew what the two missionaries only learned later—that had they remained in the air for *ten more minutes*, the petrol would have run right out. Just ten more minutes! Had it not been for that extra load, added so casually to fill in the time when the pressure gauge was being repaired, the plane would have crashed an hour ago.

How often has the situation for the children been saved by God's "extras"! There has been something almost spectacular in some of the Divine provisions for them during the past decade. When the war ended, and it became evident that the power of Communism in north China made an immediate return to Chefoo unwise, the school was opened temporarily in the Sinza

Road headquarters in Shanghai. But humid, overcrowded Shanghai was not the best place for high-spirited Western schoolchildren, however well disciplined they might be. God answered the prayers of His people by sending them up to China's most beautiful hill resort—Kuling, in the mountains of Kiangsi. A large school there, belonging to two American missions was lying empty, not having been re-occupied by them after the war. They were prepared to rent it to the C.I.M. at a very moderate figure.

For two years the children of the Mission lived happily in those spacious rented premises. But in 1949 the school was to be rented no longer. The trustees desired to dispose of the property altogether, and representatives of the Mission in North America were invited to a meeting to discuss the possibility of purchasing it.

On June 16th, 1949, therefore, the trustees for the school property on Kuling belonging to the American Episcopal and Presbyterian Missions, met Mr. Herbert Griffin, C.I.M. Home Director for North America, and Mr. George Sutherland, the treasurer. After a preliminary discussion, the chairman stated that the property and land, after reckoning U.S.$80,000 for depreciation, was valued at U.S.$100,000. Even cutting that figure in two to allow for further depreciation, the present value was estimated at U.S.$50,000. Mr. Griffin and Mr. Sutherland explained that they had no concrete offer to make, but could merely report to the General Director what sum was being asked. Then it was that they were given a figure which somewhat overwhelmed them. After twenty minutes' private discussion the trustees agreed unanimously to sell the American school on Kuling to the China Inland Mission for the sum of—U.S.$1!

U.S.$1. One American dollar! It was fantastic. It was,

of course, just a legal method of transferring ownership of the property. That neither the original owners nor the C.I.M. could hope to retain it permanently was becoming evident, it is true, but even in the light of the political situation in China it was a most generous gesture. The sale was merely conditional on the property being used as a school for the children of missionaries! So whether the time the Mission could remain in China be long or short, the need for school premises was met! The Father of mercies was answering the many urgent prayers that ascended to Him that whatever might happen in China the children should be sheltered from the storm.

Nor was the American School the only provision He made on Kuling, which for a few short years took the place that Chefoo had for so long held in the affections of parents. At Chefoo there had been a Sanatorium as well as the schools, a place to which parents flocked when holidays at the coast fell due (but once in three years for some working far away in the interior). That such a provision could be made in China's most fashionable hill resort seemed unlikely. Indeed, in 1948 the hope of returning to Communist-occupied Chefoo had not been finally dismissed. With the possibility of regaining possession of the premises there, to have laid out a large sum of money on property in Kuling would have seemed recklessly extravagant. Missionaries expect hardships, and the hardship of holidays away from their children must be accepted when necessary. Until Chefoo could be re-opened therefore, it seemed that a holiday-home near the school was out of the question.

The premises in Chefoo never were regained, but God had not forgotten that parents yearn to see their children, and that workers grown weary need refreshment. And if His stewards are not in a position to buy or rent comfortable hotels, it by no means implies that His resources are at a low ebb! And if He chooses to give a fully-equipped luxury hotel to them in answer to their earnest request for "some sort of lodgings near the children", should they refuse it?

Give them a luxury hotel He did. Fairy Glen, with its spacious rooms, family bungalows, lovely lawns and well laid out gardens was second only to one among the many beautiful hotels on Kuling. So far removed was it from anything C.I.M. missionaries were accustomed to holidaying in that when Mr. Griffin went to Kuling during a visit to China, he did no more than look at it from a distance. He had little time for mere sightseeing, and had he been on the look-out for a holiday-home for missionaries he would certainly not have thought of Fairy Glen. On his return journey to America, however, the liner on which he was travelling put in at Honolulu, and in response to a long-standing invitation he went ashore to visit friends who lived there. After a short but happy stay, he continued his journey, little knowing the plan that was being perfected with a Father's love—for it so happened that those warm-hearted friends of his college days were the owners of Fairy Glen!

It was but a month later that he heard from them. Their letter contained a startling inquiry. Could the C.I.M. make any use of Fairy Glen, they enquired, either as a school in the winter or a hostel in the summer? "If the answer is 'Yes, you want it,' " the letter continued, "arrangements can be made so that it can be put to use by September. The hotel has eighty rooms, is fully furnished at present with its own electric plant. There are several main buildings, and a number of bungalows." If it could be used, the hotel would be *given* to the Mission!

And so it came about that during the Mission's last years in China, it was provided with the most beautiful holiday-home it had ever possessed. Summer months saw Fairy Glen a centre where families were gleefully reunited and workers who were weary relaxed in the midst of unaccustomed beauty and even luxury. And when the time came for parents to descend the hill and return to dusty cities where the grip of Communism was growing tighter and tighter, and anti-foreign feeling was being stirred against them, they remembered with thankfulness the peaceful walks, the long views across tree-clad mountains, the beautiful spot so strangely remote from the turmoil on the plains, where God had placed their children. Had the school been in a populous city, or a seaport like Chefoo, what restrictions might not be placed upon the youngsters? But up on that mountain, almost isolated now, they were freer than they would have been perhaps anywhere else in China.

Fairy Glen and the American School had to be abandoned when the Mission withdrew from China. The schoolchildren were scattered, returning to their respective home countries. Their schooling must be obtained there from henceforth. But the mercy of God remained unchanged. Individual stories of scholarships gained, and help given to obtain entry into good schools would be too many to relate. The outstanding need was not so much in relation to education as to the provision of homes for the children—homes where they "belonged", where they could be cared for, where they could enjoy some sort of family life. Without them, how could parents return with free minds to the mission field?

It has been in connection with these homes, which have now been established in U.S.A., Canada, Australia and England that God's continued care and power have been most evident. Four comfortable homes with beautiful gardens and "house-parents" who are themselves members of the Mission. And some of the stories connected with their provision demonstrate that care and power so clearly, that this recital of "some of His ways" would be incomplete without them.

Mr. J. Oswald Sanders, now General Director of the Mission, was Home Director for Australia at the time when the necessity for providing a home for the children of C.I.M. missionaries there arose. On him devolved the responsibility of obtaining suitable premises. It meant starting from scratch for at first there was not even any money! Prayer was constantly made that this need might be met. When a legacy for £7,500 was received, however, it was by no means evident that this was God's answer, for the Mission field itself must come first. £5,000 was therefore sent to Singapore, and the remaining £2,500 retained for outstanding commitments at home. There was £1,500 in hand for the children's hostel, and that was all. Then Singapore returned the £5,000! There was sufficient in hand for immediate needs—let this extra £5,000 be used for a home for the children, came the word from headquarters.

£6,500. It was a fair sum, but it was not large enough to buy a house of a size sufficient to accommodate a family expanding to twenty and more members, as inquiries soon proved. £10,000 was the price of such property, and nowhere could Mr. Sanders find anything suitable below that figure. So when a house suddenly came into the market which was ideal in every respect, he had no expectation of obtaining it when he went along to the auction. He merely went to test market values! And the blank cheque he asked the Secretary for just as he was leaving the C.I.M. office was quite an afterthought. "I might as well take it, just in case the place goes cheap. . . ."

The bidding for the house opened at £5,000. It jumped to £5,500. Then to £6,000. Then to £6,250.

Then there was a slight pause. Just long enough, perhaps, for the realization to dawn that the next bid would be £6,500. The limit, as far as buying a home for the children of C.I.M. missionaries was concerned. And if no home were provided, some who were willing to go again to regions where Christ had not yet been named would be unable to go.

"Oh, Lord! . . ." A wordless, urgent prayer filled that pregnant pause. "Oh, Lord! . . ." And then he bid.

"£6,500!"

And the bidding stopped.

The auctioneer tried to coax another bid. No one responded. He could not understand it, for such property was fetching £10,000 and more. £6,750? But no one made a move. He held his hammer poised for a moment. Going for £6,500 . . . . The hammer came down. Gone for £6,500 to Mr. Sanders! The blank cheque asked for so casually at the last minute was filled in, and the house became the property of the C.I.M.

The homes in U.S.A. and Canada have quite a different history. They were both an outright gift. Mr. and Mrs. Detenbeck had set aside a large sum of money to establish Theodore, their only son, in legal practice after the war. Soon after his return from Italy, however, he had suddenly passed away. The parents, heartbroken as they were, decided that the money set aside should now be dedicated to the service of the Lord they and he loved. Was there some way in which it could be used in the C.I.M. to establish a memorial to the name of their son? Were premises needed anywhere which would perpetuate his memory?

Homes for the children of missionaries! This is the answer that has satisfied their parent hearts. In the entrance hall of a large farm-house adjoining the Prairie Bible Institute at Three Hills, Alberta, hangs a large photograph of Theodore W. Detenbeck. The children of Canadian missionaries, to whom this place with its large playing fields and vegetable gardens is "home" know his name well, and have every reason to reverence his memory as they would that of an elder brother whose Christian example they would do well to follow. And so the children of American missionaries. Their home is in the famous university town of Wheaton, U.S.A., an old-fashioned yet well-equipped mansion standing in its own grounds! They, too, have a photograph of the young U.S. Army officer in their entrance hall. They know the story of the sorrow that came to his parents when he died, and how the lovely home is the outcome of that sorrow that enlarged, rather than straitened their hearts. The home has an added value in their eyes because of it. And perhaps there is sown in their happy, childish hearts the seed of a principle to guide their own lives in years to come.

Measure thy life by loss instead of gain;
Not by the wine drunk, but the wine poured forth;
For love's strength standeth in love's sacrifice;
And whoso suffers most hath most to give.

CHAPTER FOUR

"SHALL I NOT SEEK REST FOR THEE?"

AND what about those at the other end of life to the children, who have already borne the burdens, the heat, the strain of the day, and are now approaching the exodus which will usher them into the bright realm of eternity—the retired workers? Youth and prime have been spent in "the high places of the field", but now age is taking its toll. The bodies that have been so active in the past, move slowly: the hands that were swift to stretch out and help others now grope rather uncertainly for a stronger one to grasp. And as the years move on, and weakness increases—what then? Where shall they go now, who will care for them, who will provide?

"Even to hoar hairs will I carry you." How reassuringly the words come ringing down through the years! "Whosoever shall do the will of God, the same is . . . my mother." The doing of the will of God was the goal in youth—in what manner will the promise of a personal, sacred relationship be fulfilled in old age? For very many of the retired workers are women who never heard the word "mother" addressed to them. The doing of the will of God had involved foregoing that. And now in old age, childless, who would assume that peculiar responsibility which a good son would undertake for his mother? The practical provision of a home, and care? Do the promises of God only apply to the spiritual realm? Does He who promises rest to those who come to Him think only of the soul?

Certainly not in the experience of the China Inland

Mission! Time and time again, when apparently insurmountable problems have arisen regarding retired workers and their need for a home, it had been as though Someone silently appeared on the scene, and quietly said, "This is my responsibility." And then it has become apparent that plans have already been made, a place already provided.

Such a case occurred in Australia a few years ago. Retired workers, no longer able to care for themselves, needed a home, and there was no money to buy one. But an old friend had left a house to the Mission, hoping it might be used as a mission home. Actually, it was unsuitable both in location and accommodation, and had therefore been put in the market. Just at the time when the need of the retired workers was becoming acute, and a subject of much prayer, the house was sold, realizing £3,500.

Encouraged by this timely sale, inquiries were immediately set on foot to find the market price of the type of house required. It was exactly twice as much as was in hand—£7,000! But this seeming obstacle deterred neither prayer nor diligent search, and one morning the C.I.M. Home Director saw a house advertised in a most desirable neighbourhood for £3,500. It had been put up for auction a short time previously, but since there were tenants in the house who could not, by law, be evicted, no one had bid the reserve price. A week after the auction, however, the tenants gave notice! In order to avoid further delay in winding up the estate the executors decided to sell cheaply, thus it was priced at £3,500—just the amount in hand from the sale of the house that the owner had hoped might provide a home in the Mission. And as well as being eminently suitable this property was worth about double that amount, as Mr. Sanders realized as soon as he saw it.

He was not the only one to realize its value. When he arrived, others were already looking over the house, and the occupant told him that someone who had inspected it earlier was going to buy it. That being so, the prospective purchaser might even now be on the way to the agents' office. If the race were to the swift, the C.I.M. looked like losing it!

But the race is not always to the swift. There proved to be an even quicker way than the most rapid means of transit to the agents' office, and this property, it seems, was that which God had chosen for His servants. Acting on a sudden inspiration, Mr. Sanders stepped to the nearest telephone, and rang the agents. The China Inland Mission would buy that house, he announced, and he would come round immediately with the deposit! When he arrived he learned that *between his telephone call and his appearance a short time later with the money, no less than three would-be purchasers had called*—only to be told that the property was no longer in the market! The beautiful house with its ten rooms all on one floor, ideal for old people, had already been sold to the China Inland Mission!

Houses convenient for old people, and at the same time economical to run, are not easily obtained, as mission secretaries in the home countries well know. When councils meet to decide what is required, and the price for which it must be obtained, the two never seem to harmonize! Yet experience proves again and again that these conclusions, arrived at by prayer and faith, are not impossible with God. It did not seem likely for instance, that when new property for retired workers' home and mission home in Toronto had to be obtained, the ideal of two adjacent blocks of flats with a single heating system could be obtained. Domestic arrangements would thereby be simplified, certainly, and running expenses considerably reduced—but where find two blocks of four flats each, next door to each other, and from which all the tenants would be willing to move out? Yet that is exactly what Mr. W. Tyler, after weeks of prayer and search, did find, and where Mission headquarters in Toronto are now situated. And let it be added that for some reason all the tenants in that block where the retired workers were to live moved out in good time for the whole place to be altered and prepared for moving day!

If the task of obtaining those two blocks of flats with a single heating system in Toronto was a formidable one, the practical problem that faced the Mission in Great Britain in 1953 seemed even greater. Fifty years ago the majority of C.I.M. recruits was drawn from the British Isles, with the consequence that there are more retired workers in this than any other country. The need for a larger home than the Mission already possessed was becoming urgent. It was estimated that a house large enough to accommodate about thirty people was required. Several of them could move about only with difficulty, so a lift was a necessity. The neighbourhood of Tunbridge Wells was the most desirable. And the money in hand to expend for the purpose required was very limited!

Inquiries produced a number of buildings, for large houses for sale are not so difficult to find. But they were either too old, too inconvenient, too dilapidated, too far from London or much too expensive! It seemed impossible to find a house that fulfilled all the requirements. "Ought we to *expect* to get just what we want?" The question arose at one of the Council meetings, when a further report of fruitless search for suitable property was made. There were good sound reasons for wanting just such a house, certainly, but . . . was it asking too much?

"I think we *ought* to expect it," said one member of

Council quietly. "Hudson Taylor would have done so."

The search continued. And then, quite suddenly it seemed, God drew the curtain back and disclosed a house far better than they were looking for! And He made it clear it was for them.

Rev. George Scott, now Home Director for Great Britain, was on holiday when an urgent telephone message reached him.

> There is a house which may suit you at Pembury. Others are interested but the owner will defer a decision until you have seen it. Telephone Pembury immediately.

He did so, and the following day travelled to Pembury. It is two miles from the centre of Tunbridge Wells. He walked up a wide, sweeping drive to a long, three-storeyed house whose terraced lawns ran down to a beech hedge, beyond which stretched meadows, trees and hills, right to the sky-line. It was more beautiful than anything he had dreamt of. The owner was a Christian lady who, since she had to dispose of her home, desired greatly that it should be used as a home for elderly people connected with some Christian organization, and was offering it to such at a price far below market value! And the house had a lift! It all seemed too good to be true—but it *was* true.

The lady of the house had known nothing of the China Inland Mission and the need of the retired workers when she decided to sell her house. Indeed, she had another organization in mind when first she offered the house at the very low price, and was greatly disappointed when it was unable to take it. She had almost despaired of seeing her home used in the way she desired, and had already put it in the hands of agents when one night she was suddenly awakened. The thought of the house was still in her mind, and almost as clearly as if she heard a Voice, the thought came "Write to Tom Rees". She did not know Mr. Rees, but she wrote to him the next day, asking if he knew of a Christian organization requiring such a place as Cornford House. He knew of none, but got in touch with a friend in a firm of building contractors. The friend knew of none —but his secretary did! She had heard the China Inland Mission were looking for a home for retired workers, for she had been asked a few weeks previously if she knew of such a place! And so the links in the chain were complete. The owner of Cornford House was brought in touch with C.I.M. and within a month the house became the property of the Mission.

It so happened that the income of the Mission was unusually low at this time, but money had already been contributed from various sources especially for a home for retired workers, so the purchase of the beautiful estate was possible. Extensive alterations were necessary, however, and no money could be spared from the General Fund for these. But that was not allowed to hinder matters. It became quite evident that the Lord was making Cornford House, in a peculiar way, His responsibility. Gifts *specially earmarked for the home* trickled in in a steady stream —on one occasion at a time when unexpected expenses were looming up £5,000 was received specifically "for Cornford House"! Furniture and equipment came from all sorts of unexpected sources. And when, on September 23rd, 1954, Cornford House was officially opened, every expense incurred had been met quite apart from the the General Fund of the Mission.

Had the choice of a home been left to the retired workers themselves, they would certainly not have looked for anything like the house in Pembury. Something far less imposing in a vastly inferior neighbourhood would have seemed adequate, from their point of view. But if God chose to give this generous gift, could they decline to accept it? And so His people, according to His word, dwell in a quiet and peaceable habitation.

Equally beautiful in its smaller way is the home in Winchester but the manner of its giving was different. There is a simplicity and a perfectness about this gift, which is almost sublime. It came as quietly and clearly as the evening star suddenly appears in the sky. For one day, the Secretary at C.I.M. Newington Green received a letter from a lady whose name he had never heard before and about whom he knew nothing, saying that she and her sister would like to give their home in Winchester to the Mission. Rev. Norman Pateman showed the letter to Mr. Fred Mitchell, who was then the Home Director. Together they travelled down to Winchester and saw the place that was being offered. It was a two-storeyed six-bedroomed house, with two reception rooms and a sun parlour, standing in a beautiful well kept garden on a hillside on the outskirts of the cathedral city. It was in perfect condition, charmingly furnished. It was being used as a holiday home for old ladies, but the two sisters who owned it were elderly themselves now, and wanted to ensure that the earthly home they felt they would soon be leaving for their heavenly one, would still render useful service. So they decided to give it to the C.I.M.

Mr. Mitchell and Mr. Pateman were a little taken aback. The two ladies were complete strangers, and so far as was known had had no contact with the Mission or anyone in it. Why was it they wanted to give their home to it? How did they come to know of the China Inland Mission? they were asked.

"Oh, we've always known about the C.I.M.," was the calm reply! And that was the only one they gave!

The lovely house with its large garden and its furniture was handed over some time later. Nor was that all. They had loved this home, these elderly ladies, and wanted it to be maintained in good condition after they had gone. So they handed over an investment which was to be used for the upkeep of the Winchester home, and that only! And so the upkeep of this home for six or seven retired workers costs the Mission nothing at all. Once again, it was as though a son with aging parents had silently stepped into the scene and quietly said,

"This is my responsibility."

CHAPTER FIVE

EMERGENCY HEADQUARTERS

"So the balloon has gone up at last!"

It was December 7th, 1941, and Mr. J. R. Sinton, the Deputy Director of C.I.M., was writing up his diary in Chungking. "Japanese attacked Honolulu, Manila, Hongkong early morning. . . . Expect that both U.S.A. and G.B. have declared war on Japan. It was a knockout, although so long expected, and means the 'skeleton' must get clothes and breath."

The "Skeleton" was the name laughingly given to the little party of four men and women who exactly a year ago had left Shanghai for Chungking to be ready for just such an emergency as this. For twelve months they had been living in the city that was to become famous as "China's wartime capital", actively engaged in evangelistic and church work, but always with the realization that some day they might find themselves the headquarters of the Mission, to whom some 700 missionaries scattered throughout Free China would look for direction in their work—and for the channelling of financial supplies! And now it had happened. Little wonder that Mr. Sinton added in his diary entry, "We seemed to be somewhat stupefied all day."

Humanly speaking, the blow could scarcely have fallen at a more inopportune moment. It was the last month of the quarter, the time when money was transmitted from the home countries to Mission headquarters, from there to be disbursed throughout the field. If that money had already been remitted, it would mean that the money would be all tied up in Shanghai, while the new headquarters in Chungking must try to supply the needs of over 700 missionaries from a quite inadequate fund.

Now the Japanese attack on Pearl Harbour was politically unforeseen, even by those who knew better than anyone else how tense the situation had become. It is inconceivable that the British and American ambassadors would have allowed the C.I.M. schools, with their hundreds of American and British children to remain in Chefoo, a Japanese occupied port, had they anticipated the turn that events would take. Much less, therefore, had the Mission leaders any grounds for changing the practice of sending money to the field early in the last month of the quarter. So, of course, they arranged to do so as usual. What was, however, hidden from ambassadors and admirals, missionaries and men, was all crystal clear to God. In remarkable ways He saw to it that funds reached those for whom they were intended, in spite of political upheavals.

Early in December the treasurer in Philadelphia, Mr. George Sutherland, prepared to forward funds from the United States to Shanghai. On December 6th, little knowing what would happen in the Pacific within the next few hours, he sent U.S.$9,750 to the Chase National Bank in New York, to be cabled immediately—to Shanghai.

He might well have gone a day or two earlier. The possibility of war being declared between the Allies and Japan was ever in the minds of the Mission leaders, and funds were therefore being forwarded to the field more frequently than usual, lest the channels should close and missionaries in China be left short of cash. Had he gone one day earlier, the money so urgently needed in Chungking would have been tied up in Shanghai. But he sent the cheques on the 6th, not the 5th, of the month, and by the time they were received in New York, the news had just been received that war had broken out. The Chase National Bank awaited further instructions from the C.I.M. With immeasurable thankfulness that the money had not been forwarded to Shanghai, the bank was instructed to send the money to Chungking instead.

The case of the £5,000 from Britain was even more remarkable. At the beginning of the second world war the British Government put a restriction on the amount of money that could be sent out of the country. Missionary societies were allowed a fixed quota, and more than that could not be sent. In the autumn of 1941, however, an appeal was made that the sum might be increased in view of the rise of the cost of living in China, and the C.I.M. obtained permission in November to forward £5,000 above the quota. Joyfully it was sent to the Bank of England to be sent immediately to Shanghai. And had everything gone smoothly, the money would have been received in Shanghai and promptly "frozen" for the duration of war.

Everything did not go smoothly. The Bank of England encountered a technical hitch. Just what the hitch was the Mission probably never knew. As far as C.I.M. is concerned, like Jonah's whale, it was prepared of God. The money was held up for several days by that hitch. The early days of December were ticked off the calendar, and still the money could not be forwarded. Not until after December 7th did the "hitch" get smoothed out. Then things went smoothly enough, and in due course £5,000 was forwarded—not to be frozen in Shanghai after all, but to be put to good use by the "skeleton" staff in Chungking.

Such experiences at the outset of taking over responsibility were very reassuring. In addition to the transmissions that had surely been Divinely delayed, there was the fact that Mr. Frank Parry in Shanghai had sent out remittances to all missionaries a month earlier than usual —only a few days before the undeclared war broke out. Everyone on the field was thus personally provided for for three months to come! How evident it was that a Mastermind was behind it all! The future was hidden from those who waited on God, just as it was from those who feared Him not; but those who looked to Him to guide were not put to shame. Guide them He did, even though often enough they were unaware of it at the time. To the little group in Chungking it was a heartening realization indeed that "He that is perfect in knowledge is with thee". On the last day of the year, always observed throughout the Mission as a day of prayer, the treasurer in Chungking was able to announce that the best part of a million Chinese dollars was available for use in Free China.

"We feel greatly encouraged as we go forward", wrote Mr. Sinton in his diary. Then he added, with the candour of one who commits his thoughts to paper with no anticipation of other eyes than his own seeing them, "although if we knew all that is before us we should probably refuse to face it!"

Merciful indeed it was that the future was veiled. The years that lay ahead were dangerous, feverish years, with news constantly reaching headquarters of missionaries hastily evacuating stations, or else being cut off by advancing Japanese armies. It was not long before the only way out of China was over the hazardous Burma Road, and when eventually even that route was cut the problem of getting workers whose health broke down to the homelands was a grave one. This uncertainty, with its attendant strain on top of the normal burdens and hardships of missionary life in inland China might well have proved more than enough to bear. But there was something else that was ever at hand to oppress—twin monsters that seemed to draw nearer and nearer, threatening to squeeze the very life out of the Mission in Free China.

Very practical monsters, they were, affecting such necessities as food and clothing, reducing larders and gnawing into trunks. They put faith to the test those years, the monsters of Inflation and a Pegged Exchange. The cost of living went spiralling dizzily upwards, as the value of the Chinese dollar dropped. One missionary, for instance, had to pay a servant as much each month as would have been sufficient to employ him for four and a half years before the war! Little wonder that many missionaries had to stop employing servants at all, and learned to live cheaper than coolies! For however much the Chinese dollar depreciated in value in China itself, from the point of view of the Allies it remained the same. The exchange was pegged. Month after month £1 bought only a fraction more than 77 Chinese dollars, irrespective of the fact that 77 Chinese dollars would not purchase a quarter of what they did when the exchange rate was first fixed. Foreign firms and organizations working in China had to bear the brunt of this effort by the Allies to stabilize the rapidly depreciating value of Chinese currency. The "Black Market" flourished in those days, for if an American dollar only exchanged officially for some 25 Chinese dollars, it exchanged for considerably more when the official eye was turned elsewhere—or conveniently closed! Many were taking advantage of that strangely affected official eye, and there must have been times when the path of righteousness and scrupulous honesty in business dealings was trodden not without an inward struggle on the part of those at Emergency headquarters who knew that the remittances they were sending out to missionaries on the field were quite inadequate to meet their needs. At a time when skilled Chinese workmen were earning $60 per day, for instance, missionaries in the same city received but $20.

"The cost of living is getting worse and worse", wrote the treasurer at Chungking. "Potatoes here are 1*s*. 2*d*. per lb. We are practically vegetarians. But our lot at Emergency headquarters, with two women servants and a male cook for the sixteen or eighteen of us is unquestionably better than many of our fellow-workers who are servantless. This is a most serious situation—health will be impaired, we fear, with so little meat and milk, and the work is bound to suffer when all household duties in this land without labour-saving devices have to be done by the inexperienced missionaries themselves. There is very little of complaint, but the factual letters we receive speak volumes. Our prayer is unceasing that soon we may receive a fair deal in the matter of exchange, for herein lies the trouble. Here is just one example. Mr. Gould priced a pair of Viyella socks two days ago—$400, equalling £5!"

That letter was written on March 17th, 1943. For over a year prices had been rising while the rate of exchange remained the same. And although the Mission's income had increased during the year, in the remarkable way it seems always to do as the needs increase, still when the money was changed into Chinese currency it proved only sufficient to pay all expenses leaving very little over for remittances to the missionaries themselves.

Perhaps it should be explained that one of the most rigid financial principles of the Mission is never to go into debt. For this reason, any commitments for rent, mission employees and similar expenses must always be met first. It is understood also that expenses connected with the continuation of the work, such as money required for itinerations, are among the high priorities. Indeed, the lowest of all "priorities" is the personal remittances to missionaries. And this leads to another principle, more vital even than that of not going into debt. It is the principle that every member of the Mission looks direct to God for material supplies. "Every member of the Mission is expected to recognize that his dependence for the supply of his need is on God, who called him, and for whom he works, and not on the human organization." It is only men and women with a practical, living faith who will join the Mission on this understanding, and only such men and women would be happy in its fellowship. So although the money received in the General Fund is equally divided amongst all, Directors receiving no more than the youngest missionary, it is recognized that personal remittances can only be drawn from what remains when other claims have been met. And when those remittances prove to be insufficient, it is but an opportunity to put God to the test, who has promised "Seek ye first the kingdom of God and His righteousness, and all these things shall be added unto you."

When Hudson Taylor was working out the basis on which the Mission should be built, the "Principles and Practice" to which all those joining it must subscribe, he wrote concerning the attitude of missionaries towards their material needs,

"Their faith must be in God, their expectation from Him. The funds might fail, or the Mission might cease to exist; but if they put their trust in Him, He will never fail nor disappoint them."

During those war years the funds did fail, though not because contributions diminished. It was a constant source of thankful wonder to see how, in spite of the hardships and privations imposed on those in the homelands by the world war, the Mission's income increased. In 1943 £80,000 *more* was received in the various home countries than in 1940. But inflation and the pegged exchange meant that the income in Free China was, of itself, inadequate. And so those who in all the enthusiasm and confidence of youth had signed the "Principles and Practice" of the Mission, thereby asserting their readiness, among other things, to trust God for the supply of their material needs, found themselves face to face with a situation which demanded they should do so. The following chapter will give glimpses of some of the ways in which He responded to their faith.

CHAPTER SIX

RAVENS IN CHINA

"HAVE you any flour?" demanded the Japanese officer peremptorily.

"Yes," replied the young woman missionary.

"Give it to me," he said roughly. She turned and led the way to her cupboard. The officer followed her, watching closely as she opened the door. What food-stuffs were stored away in this Englishwoman's home? He had a company of men to provide for, and the deserted city had already been ransacked. It was in the days before the Pearl Harbour outrage, but although compounds occupied by Americans and Europeans were inviolate, international law demanding that they should be protected, this was a case of need for him. Apart from two or three old women who had been left behind when everyone else fled, this woman missionary and her colleague, and the Chinese employees on their compound were the only people left in the city. They must have a store of food hidden away somewhere, and he was determined to get hold of it.

The cupboard looked strangely empty. A few jars and bottles. . . . "I want flour!"

The missionary picked up one of the jars and handed it to him. He looked inside, and then angrily at her. She was making fun of him! The jar contained little more than a pound of flour.

"Is this all you've got?" he asked.

"Yes," she replied. "I don't know where to get any more."

The officer looked around, peered into the other jars,

and after satisfying himself that there really was no more flour than that pound in the bottom of the jar, said, "That's no good to a company of men," and walked off. The following day his superior officer, with the charming courtesy of the Orient which Westerners sometimes find a little difficult to fathom, called at the mission house and presented the occupants with a tin of pineapple chunks! He had heard, he said, that they were short of food!

Very grateful they were for that tin of pineapple chunks. Their diet those days was composed mainly of millet and what weeds they found to be edible. Their stores were reduced to a minimum—millet, and that one lb. of flour into which they dipped very sparingly, reserving it for special occasions. Boiled millet three times a day becomes very monotonous after a time, and when, one day, they were standing at their compound gates watching Japanese soldiers laden with big, fresh turnips returning from a forage in the neighbouring countryside, their mouths watered. Turnips!

"Pray they may drop one!" said the missionary to her companion, half laughingly. How wonderful it would be to have turnip for supper!

The Heavenly Father's mercies are very tender. They did have turnip for supper. A large turnip rolled off the armful a Japanese soldier was carrying, just as he was passing the compound gate. Neither he nor his companions paid any heed to it, and there on the ground it lay until one of the missionaries thankfully went and picked it up. That turnip helped to provide a meal the two women never forgot.

They were marooned in that city for over three months, and only once were they able to buy food—four lb. of potatoes and a dozen eggs on an occasion when they obtained permission to go and preach in a village a mile or so from the city. The millet and the flour had nearly run out by that time. But just before it did, fellow-missionaries from whom they had been cut off got through the lines and brought them out in safety. The barrel of meal had not failed. "We praised the Lord who had not forgotten His children there in the loess hills, and who provided them with daily food in a time when many were starving."

Another little story demonstrating the intimate loving-kindness of the Lord, comes from a city also in the north of China that was besieged by the Japanese. In this case also it lay empty, except for the compound where two or three missionary families were living. They had laid in, as best they could, a store of grain to provide themselves with flour, the staff of life. But they had little else besides when one morning, shortly after an air raid, a missionary baby put in her appearance! And although the tiny mite was promptly put under the bed as the sound of aeroplanes was heard again, it was not so much the thought of bombs dropping that worried the nurse as the much more mundane problem of how to provide suitable food for the baby's mother. There remained little more in the cupboard now than flour. Eggs, vegetables, fruit, meat were unobtainable in this beleaguered city. Oh to be able to make tasty, nourishing broths for the mother of the newly-born babe, for the first few days at least! But it was out of the question. There was simply nothing to make the broths of!

And then it happened—the little personal miracle that meant as much to the missionary community in that Chinese city as did the visits of the ravens to Elijah by the brook Cherith. For a *chicken* flew right over the twenty-foot high wall and landed with a plomp inside the compound! Where it came from, they never knew. On the other side of the wall stretched field after field of corn-stalks, with no human habitation from whence the chicken would have strayed. In any case, all the Chinese families except those on the mission compound had departed—and when Chinese families depart they leave surprisingly little behind them! Certainly not chickens! No one on the compound claimed this one, and after inquiries as to its owner had proved fruitless, it became nourishing, tasty broths for the mother of the newly-born babe for some days to come!

About the same time, but in very different surroundings, missionary parents with four small children returning to England and delayed in Canada owing to war conditions, suddenly found themselves penniless. The furnished house which had been so wonderfully provided for them was broken into, and all their money stolen. Apart from a small supply of groceries and a few coppers they had in their pockets, they had nothing—and it was several weeks before they could expect their next remittance!

Very earnestly the young couple made their petitions to their Heavenly Father that night. This was a test of faith indeed—and a test of God's faithfulness. How would He meet their needs now?

They were soon to see!

The following day a box of provisions was delivered at their door. There was no indication from whom it had come, but the bill was paid, and the goods addressed to them. *That* gift saw them through the next two or three days, and then a letter arrived for them from a friend in England—containing a cheque!

Now, as it happened, financial restrictions had been imposed in England, forbidding that money should be sent out of the country privately. The missionaries' friend, however, knew nothing of these restrictions, and sent the cheque in good faith. The missionaries knew nothing about them, either, and went joyfully to the bank to cash the cheque. The most remarkable fact in this story, perhaps, is that not even the bank clerk knew of the new regulations. He cashed the cheque without demur! Not until some weeks later was the mistake discovered. The missionaries were required to refund the money, forwarded to them in error. But by that time they were in a position to do so, having received their quarterly remittance. That innocent mistake had been God's provision to meet the emergency caused by the theft!

Emergencies! Emergencies were constantly arising in those days, especially in China, when sudden Japanese advances necessitated hasty evacuations. See, for instance, a party of missionaries, some with bicycles laden with suitcases and bundles, others, grey-haired women among them, walking out of the city from which streamed thousands of Chinese—refugees like themselves. The Japanese were coming, and it was every man for himself. The lorries that rumbled along past the hurrying multitudes were so laden that they looked like slowly moving masses of human beings, clinging to each other to avoid being shaken off. To obtain a passage on those lorries was impossible, as the senior man missionary discovered after hours of searching. No money could buy one.

"There's nothing else for it," he said at last. "We'll have to go as best we can. We can't wait any longer. Those who haven't bicycles will have to walk. They may be able to get a lift on the road. . . . We must go at once."

They started. One of them rose weakly from a sick bed to mount her bicycle and ride, wobbling, over the uneven ground out of the city. For days they straggled along with the swarm of refugees, sleeping where they could find so much as a roof to shelter them. Lorries with their loads of human freight lumbered past, their drivers heeding not the hands appealingly held out to stop them. "No more room—no more room", and they drove on.

One day one of the grey-haired missionaries in that straggling group knew she could go no further. She looked at the steep hill that lay ahead, and her heart sank. She had not the strength to climb it. The other walkers and the cyclists with their laden machines were on ahead of her, and in any case, they could not have helped. But when, at eventide, they realized she was missing, some would refuse to go on. "I shall hold them up," she thought, feeling rather desperate. And the Japanese were close behind. . . .

Suddenly she remembered something she had read in one of Oswald Chambers' books.

"Lord, show Thyself sufficient for this crisis now."

It had impressed her at the time, and now it came to mind with quiet power. "Lord, show Thyself sufficient for *this* crisis, *now*."

And at that moment a lorry came slowly into sight, around a bend in the road. "This is it," she thought.

It was over-laden, of course. There seemed no reason to suppose that she would obtain a place on it, that *her* uplifted hand would gain a response more than the hundreds of other uplifted hands the lorry must have passed along the way. Nevertheless, with that quick, confident prayer in her heart, she raised it. Now should she see how God would be proved.

A tall Chinese man slithered down from the lorry to the ground and came towards her.

"We can't stop," he said courteously. "But we are going slowly enough for you to get on. Let me help you. . . ."

It was amazing. He asked no questions, demanded no money, just helped her up as friendly hands stretched down to grasp hers.

"There's another white-haired woman walking a bit further on," said the missionary to her unknown friend.

"We will take her on too," he said. And they did!

The lorry rumbled on—slowly overtaking the others of the party who were on bicycles proceeding slowly with their heavy loads.

"Tom, Tom!" called the missionary as she saw them. "Throw up the suitcases—throw them up here!" The senior man missionary took in the situation promptly after his momentary surprise, and delayed not to throw up the suitcases! "How wonderful," thought the woman, waving cheerfully as the lorry passed her friends. "I thought I should hold them up, and now, instead, I'm *helping* them!"

The lorry belonged to the Salt Gabelle, and the tall Chinese official in charge was one who had in the past received kindness from English people which he never forgot. He was ever ready to befriend any whom he met. Probably from no other source would the aid that money could not buy have been forthcoming, but from that one man. And even he might have passed her by, had not the swift reminder of God's sufficiency for any crisis prompted her to stand forward and hold up her hand.

That same missionary group reached a city where they knew no one. They were housed and fed on the compound of hospitable missionaries whose accommodation was already crowded with refugees. But their money was all spent, and they had little more than the clothes they stood up in—grimy, crumpled clothes in which they had travelled over muddy roads and slept in dirty inns. It might take weeks before they could get money sent through to them from the Emergency headquarters in Chungking. And they had immediate, intimate, personal needs that required a little ready cash right on the spot! They made those little personal needs known to God, and there in that Chinese city in which they were complete strangers, He supplied them. A Chinese gentleman met one of the missionaries one day and said he had heard there were some China Inland Mission workers who had arrived as refugees.

"I never met any myself," he said, "but a friend of mine knows several, and has told me about them. If they are refugees, they must be needing money. I should like to help them." And he gave them 100 Chinese dollars each!

God's ravens in those days were often Chinese. The practical sympathy and help they gave when they realized their missionary friends were short of money many a time made just the difference between inadequacy and sufficiency. A dozen eggs, a chicken, a basket of fresh vegetables—such gifts found their way into mission stations too often to be numbered. "Wang Tai-tai came... and gave us $400. First money we have ever received from Chinese", a missionary entered in her diary one evening in the early days of 1944, when funds were at their lowest. And similar records were being made in almost every province where the Mission was at work. It was worth being short of funds to become the recipients of these gifts of love from those they had come to serve. "Not because I desire a gift," wrote the great missionary 1,900 years ago. "But I desire fruit that may abound to your account. . . ." Not a few accounts of Chinese Christians abounded with such fruit.

Nor were these the only ways in which provisions came.

"Teacher, the water carrier wants to know if you have any empty kerosene tins to sell him." The missionary's servant, a willing middle-man, comes forward with the suggestion which somehow had never occurred to his mistress. Sell those old kerosene tins? For how much? The middle-man mentions a price which sounds fantastically high, but the water carrier pays it with the minimum of oriental bargaining, and comes later to see if there are any more at the same price!

"Teacher, there is a general's wife who wants to buy a foreign stove. . . ." Surely not that old one, discarded long ago because fuel was far too expensive? Would anybody be able to afford to use it in these hard times? But yes—the general's wife has plenty of money, and is delighted to buy a stove which was made in America. The missionary, inwardly exultant at this unexpected method whereby her prayers for sufficient money to meet her needs are being answered, parts with the stove rusting in the lumber-shed, without regret. And as the months roll by, goes again and again to the lumber room or her trunks, to produce a tin box, a leather case, a blanket, a woollen cardigan, something for which she discovers there is a ready market. For in those days, when the Japanese had succeeded in cutting China's avenues of supplies, foreign commodities were at a premium, and many were the missionaries whose surplus clothing and household utensils were turned into the money needed to buy "our daily bread". And when, in 1944, Japanese advances forced missionaries in Honan and Anhwei to evacuate hundreds of miles westward, many of them instead of jettisoning furniture and property on the mission stations they must leave vacant, sold it outright. The cash those quick sales provided paid for many a meal, and many a night's lodging on the long, rough journey to the far west—and relieved the treasurer at Chungking of some problems, too! In allocating the quarterly income, he had not allowed for the expenses involved in the sudden evacuation of nearly a fifth of the Mission's personnel in Free China!

For some who had to travel from the coastal province of Chekiang to the far west, and whose property had already been lost during Japanese invasions, however, to start out was like stepping into a void. Two women missionaries who set out to cross five or six provinces, on a route completely strange to them both, knew full well that they had insufficient money. But even before they commenced their journey they received a "token for good" in the shape of a gift generously given them by the Chinese Christians. In addition, a Chinese lady whom they knew insisted on providing them with their first three days' transport—by wheelbarrow, that being the local method of locomotion! One long day's motor travel was provided by American marines whom they happened to meet on the way. A Sunday's board bill in a hostel was mysteriously settled by an anonymous friend, and then, with a vast stretch of bandit-infested country ahead, they fell in with a British military mission which brought them right through, providing them with five days' free travel!

Still more remarkable was the provision made for another missionary in Chekiang who was obviously ill, yet unable to obtain medical attention. Her fellow-worker suspected it was a malignant growth—as, indeed, it proved to be. But China had been cut in half when the Japanese captured the whole of the railroad that ran from Peking via Hankow to Canton—and they were in the area that was now completely surrounded by Japanese. Humanly speaking, there seemed no way out. Hundreds of miles of overland travel from east to west China—an air trip the only way to get out to India—and then oceans to cross to America, at a time when sea passages for civilians were almost unobtainable. But truly, "Omnipotence hath servants everywhere". Within a matter of weeks she was in the famous Mayo clinic in America, recovering from an operation, successfully performed by surgeons who refused to accept a fee!

This is how it happened. The U.S. Air Force had bases in that part of China that was cut off, and were constantly flying over the lines. In one of their planes the two missionaries were flown to Kunming in west China, and from there out to Calcutta. Calcutta was a city of refugees.

Refugees from Burma, refugees from Singapore and Malaya, refugees from China. Thousands of English and American business people and missionaries had been waiting for months for passages to return to their own countries. What hope had an unknown missionary from China of getting to America immediately, even though the X-ray had revealed her condition to be serious? Nevertheless, she did. After very earnest prayer she and her companion went, armed with an introduction from a doctor in China, to see no less a person than the chief U.S. Medical Officer in Calcutta. The outcome of that interview was that the invalid was given a free passage home on an American Army plane—the first American woman to be flown home from India.

What shall we say more? Time would fail us to tell fully, for instance, of the conference of thirty workers in a tribal area, who had been living for months on the coarsest of food. How those responsible for catering for that conference would have loved to provide some delicious "extras"—but they had no stores left, and money only sufficient for that same coarse local food. Yet throughout the days of that conference they all had coffee (real coffee, not the kind they made themselves by roasting grain) and cream (Carnation cream from tins, not the synthetic sort with an acrid, salty flavour they sometimes concocted from soya beans) and cheese! Incredible, undreamed of luxuries! An American Army officer on whose vehicle Mr. Sinton had obtained a lift to the conference had, almost as an afterthought, asked him,

"What is your food situation? Got any coffee—cream—cheese?" and given him a generous supply to take along with him.

It was mainly through the good offices of American soldiers that the group of German C.I.M. Associate missionaries who were interned in Nanfeng obtained their provisions. When Nanfeng was cut off by the Japanese, the only way in which the Mission headquarters at Chungking could send relief money to their German brethren was when friendly Americans flying across the lines undertook to deliver it.

There were, however, long periods when no such messengers were available, and during one of those periods the German group found themselves at the end of their resources. In vain did they look for planes from the west. If any came, they brought no provisions for them, and when, one day, a plane arrived from the *east*, carrying evacuating missionaries, there was no cause to believe that practical help would be forthcoming from them. Evacuating missionaries were usually in need of it themselves! But this was just another example of the Heavenly Father's perfect timing. Mr. and Mrs. Hutchinson and Miss Loosley were on that plane, and before he had left the mission station which must be abandoned, Mr. Hutchinson had actually been able to sell the property. He arrived in Nanfeng with enough money to succour those German fellow-missionaries in their internment for many a long day. Little did either he or they realize fully the Divine providence that was in operation, or how completely "My times are in Thy hands". When Mr. Hutchinson said a cordial farewell to his German friends, and boarded the plane again, he no longer had the money. Gladly and promptly had he handed over that truly God-sent provision—an act that proved to be the last in a lifetime of cheerful service. The journey so wonderfully timed to bring life-sustaining succour to his fellow-workers brought him swiftly and painlessly to his long-desired haven. The plane crashed a short time after leaving Nanfeng, and all on board were killed outright.

Perhaps the most remarkable individual story of that

whole war period is that of the Preedy family. It is far too long to attempt to relate here, for it covers a period of over three years in the Philippines during the Japanese occupation. Mr. and Mrs. Preedy and their two little girls were caught in Manila, en route for their first furlough, when the Japanese attacked Pearl Harbour, and shortly afterwards invaded the Philippines. For some reason, the Preedys were not interned with the other "enemy nationals", but were left to fend for themselves in a country in which they had no previous connections, and in which an alien nation was in control! Many were the times when they literally did not know where their next meal would come from. Yet when eventually the Philippine Islands were liberated the Preedy family, including the baby boy who had been born to them, were all alive and well. During the whole three years there was only one period, lasting three days, when Mr. and Mrs. Preedy (not the children) had nothing at all to eat. As those three days were just prior to the arrival of the victorious American forces, they merely served to enhance the joys of being liberated! The Preedys never went hungry after that! The fuller story of God's provision for this little family has been told elsewhere, but this record of His power to care for His own during those years of war would seem incomplete without reference to it.

And so, in various places, and in differing degrees, those who had gone to China on the understanding that they must put their faith and expectation in God, and not in the Mission, to meet their needs, proved His willingness and ability to do so. Although provisions were sometimes supplied in what seemed to be the nick of time, and with almost dramatic suddenness, more usually they came along before shortage was acute. And perhaps one of the oft-overlooked mercies of those days was the way in which appetites were changed to accommodate themselves to supplies! Coarse food proved to be, after all, tastier and more easily digested than most people realized!

To assert, however, that C.I.M. missionaries always abounded and never suffered want would be a distortion of the truth. "I have learned," wrote the apostle Paul, "in whatsoever state I am, therewith to be content. I know both how . . . to be full and to be hungry, both to abound and to suffer need." There were few indeed who were not called upon to suffer need in some form or other. But it is probably true to say of all that their poverty proved more fruitful spiritually than fulness had been. It was the platform on which they were called to demonstrate the faith they had often asserted—that "Christ in me" is sufficient for any circumstance into which God may lead. And if there were times when faith wavered, God's faithfulness did not. For "If we believe not, yet He abideth faithful. He cannot deny Himself."

CHAPTER SEVEN

THE PEGGED EXCHANGE

THE sun was shining through a sky hazy with heat. The range of hills outside Chungking on which the C.I.M. bungalows stood rose sharply from the undulating plains leading to the Kweichow mountains, yet even up there the air seemed still and heavy. From the rooms that opened out on to the verandahs came the sound of clicking typewriters, however, and every now and then someone walked briskly from one room to another, letter in hand, intent on business. The Emergency headquarters staff moved up from the enervating heat of the Yangtze valley during the summer months to work as usual, and on this particular morning in June, 1944, there were the customary sights and sounds of activity—except in a corner of the financial department, where the treasurer, Mr. F. E. Keeble, was sitting at his desk.

It was not often that he sat there doing apparently nothing, especially when the turn of the quarter was at hand. This was the time when remittances were usually prepared and despatched to all parts of the field, and well he knew that rarely had they been more needed. At the commencement of the previous quarter he had only been able to send out half of what seemed necessary for missionaries to live on, in spite of unusually large donations from the U.S.A.

"This will mean hard going for many," he had written in a private letter to London headquarters. "Expenses these days come with a sickening thud. Excuse the term, but I really mean it. Only to-day, to hire a boat from

Chungking to Langchung for the Camerons with some freight for the hospital, has cost $60,000 (about £400 at the rate of exchange allowed, for a journey of less than 300 miles in a small native sailing boat). No one who has never experienced inflation of currency can understand what it feels to be faced with such conditions plus a pegged exchange." The same letter expressed a cheerful confidence, "However, the Lord will care for His children's need", and as he sat at his desk now he knew that the Lord was doing so. The heavy expenses that had been incurred by the unforeseen evacuation of missionaries from the two provinces of Honan and Anhwei were being met in equally unforeseen ways, and through the past months there had been ample evidence that the "Treasurer above" had resources unknown to the Mission treasurer in the hill bungalows outside Chungking. So although £8, when converted into Chinese money, was just sufficient to buy one typewriter ribbon, and £14 a pair of leather shoes, there seemed no reason to delay having the money waiting in the bank in Calcutta transmitted to Chungking, and from there remitted as speedily as possible to the field, before its value depreciated still further. And yet, as he sat there at his desk, he felt strangely restrained from doing what was, on the face of it, the only thing to be done.

For nearly two years now he had been praying that a more realistic exchange might be granted. Only recently he had changed £23,000 and received Chinese money with the equivalent of only £3,000 purchasing value to it. If he changed the money lying safely in sterling and U.S. dollars that was waiting to be transmitted, adequate as the sum would have been in normal circumstances, he knew that it would be sufficient to supply less than half of what was needed. The remittance sent out would be even smaller than the previous one. And the galling thing was that of itself the money that had been contributed, in many cases at real sacrifice, was ample for the needs of the coming quarter.

It was as much for the sake of the donors as for himself and the other members of the Mission that he was loath to change that money. Some of the smallest gifts received were the most precious, and the Lord who sat by the temple treasury in days gone by just as surely sat by the Mission treasury now, noting the willing offerings of poor and rich alike. That He would allow them to be continually reduced in value, when the needs on the field were becoming so acute, seemed incredible. Somehow, as he sat there this June morning, Fred Keeble could not believe that He would.

"Harry!" he said suddenly, looking across the desk to his colleague. Harry Gould, a sturdy Australian, looked up. "I don't feel we ought to change that money yet. With the exchange still pegged like this, it won't be half enough. What do you think?"

The two men looked at each other across the wide desk. They both knew what it would mean if they delayed. They knew that fellow-workers in isolated towns scattered throughout Free China were already getting to "the bottom of the barrel". Stores of grain were running out, supplies of firing getting low, while the price of eggs, vegetables, fruit, meat was rising higher almost every day. Some might well be without any ready cash by this time, living on what they had in store—and how little that was likely to be! To delay exchanging that money lying in the bank in Calcutta, and sending it off, decimated though it be, was a heavy responsibility at such a time. And yet. . . .

"No," said Harry Gould deliberately. "I don't think so, either."

"Let's pray about it," said Fred Keeble. They bowed

their heads and prayed, quietly but urgently, as they had prayed many times before, that the Lord would overrule the financial arrangements of earthly governments, and graciously grant His servants a better rate of exchange. Then they turned their attention to other matters. For what was probably the first time in Mission history, remittances were not sent out at the turn of the quarter.

A day or two later a letter was received from a large commercial firm trading in China, offering to take over the Mission's foreign currencies at double the rate of exchange granted in the authorized market.

In obedience to the Scriptural injunctions to "render unto Caesar the things which are Caesar's" and to obey every ordinance of man for the Lord's sake, such transactions had hitherto been resolutely avoided. The situation, however, had become so serious, that it seemed some revision of the Mission's policy not to exchange currency except through the recognized channels was necessary. The Black Market was being used so flagrantly and in so many cases by the officials of the very country on whose behalf the exchange had been fixed, that it seemed unrealistic in the extreme to abide by a law which was being broken every day with impunity. This offer from the commercial firm was very different from the usual Black Market, where far better rates could be obtained without difficulty. Was it God's answer to the many prayers that had ascended to Him for a better rate of exchange?

Mr. Keeble went along the verandah and across the courtyard to the room where Bishop Frank Houghton was working, and explained the situation to him.

"Are you, as the General Director of the C.I.M. prepared to authorize me, the treasurer of the C.I.M. to deal in this non-official market?" he asked.

Bishop Houghton answered with caution.

"Do you, as treasurer of the C.I.M. advise me, the General Director of the C.I.M. to take this step?" he inquired.

"Yes," said the treasurer, after a momentary pause. "I feel the time has come to take action." So permission was granted.

Nevertheless, the treasurer was still not quite at ease. He thought of those fellow-workers in far away towns and cities who would be eagerly looking for the remittances which would enable them to buy what was so sorely needed. How surprised they would be at the unusual delay! He longed to take advantage of this offer which had come so unexpectedly and so unsought, whereby he would be able to send them nearly twice as much as he had at first thought possible. Twice as much would still not be sufficient, as far as could be estimated, but how much better than the pathetically small sum possible if the authorized market were used! But still something restrained him, though he had permission to accept the offer. He talked it over with Mr. Gould, and they decided that before going any further in the matter they would go and ask the advice of the British Commercial Attaché in Chungking. If he sanctioned it, they would hesitate no longer.

Together they set out to walk as quickly as possible the five miles to Chungking. Across the fields they went, down the crowded, narrow road with its paved steps like a gigantic stairway that ran down the steep hillside to the river; over on the steam ferry, and then a climb up through the streets and steep lanes of the city to the white buildings over which fluttered the Union Jack.

The difficulties of the present financial situation were well known at the Consulate. Fresh requests for increased funds were constantly being sent to the Government at home as expenses increased with the rising prices. How did these missionaries, who had no Government to which they could apply, contrive to exist? The Consul General himself had sent for the C.I.M. treasurer on one occasion and asked him point-blank how they could possibly manage. "Why!" he remarked, "if this sort of condition obtained in England there'd be a revolution!" The Commercial Attaché, therefore, listened to them with sympathy, and raised no objection to the proposed use of the non-official market. Nevertheless, he advised them to have nothing to do with it. Some important developments were pending, he hinted. It would be well to wait awhile.

The two men returned to the bungalows on the hill, questioning in their minds what it all meant. Could it be that their prayer for a better rate of exchange was to be answered now?

They were not left long in doubt. A message was received from the British Ambassador to China himself, Sir Horace Seymour. He was calling a meeting of the representatives of British military and diplomatic missions, and Mr. Keeble and Mr. Gould were invited to attend to represent British missionary societies.

They attended. Sir Horace Seymour outlined the present financial situation, already well known to the twenty-five men who had gathered, and went on to say that it was impossible for British taxpayers to continue to finance diplomatic and military missions in China at the pegged rate of exchange. A financial expert had therefore come out from England to propose a method whereby the problem could be solved. He was then introduced and invited to outline the scheme whereby sterling could be exchanged for Chinese currency at a much more favourable rate.

The proposed scheme, of course, was primarily intended for diplomatic and military missions, in China on Government service. It was obviously not intended to facilitate private individuals or commercial enterprises to remain in China. The two missionaries sat quietly listening. Their affairs had not yet been mentioned. That they had been invited for a purpose they knew, but just what was it?

Sir Horace Seymour turned to the man on his right.

"Mr. Keeble," he said. "Do you think that missionary societies also would be happy to avail themselves of this avenue of exchange?"

Would missionary societies be happy to avail themselves of this avenue of exchange? What words can express the overwhelming relief at this offer? The scheme outlined was one that would increase the value of sterling by some 300 per cent.! If the singing of hearts were audible to mortal ears, the room would have resounded with the doxology! But singing hearts were hidden behind impassive faces, as the C.I.M. treasurer turned gravely to his colleague, his eyebrows slightly raised. Would missionary societies be happy to avail themselves of this avenue of exchange? His colleague, equally grave, looked at him and then nodded solemnly. The C.I.M. treasurer turned back to answer the Ambassador's question.

"Yes, sir," he said simply. . . .

After that events followed swiftly. An organization was set up whereby all British missionary societies at work in Free China could exchange their sterling at more favourable rates. Mr. Gould was nominated and seconded to act as liaison between the Embassy and all British missionary societies in China. With the added responsibility the members of the C.I.M. financial department worked harder than ever before—"but it was abundantly worthwhile!" And at last the delayed remittances were sent out, an ample provision for the needs of the coming quarter. The strain was lifted.

"We sailed in much calmer waters financially thereafter," wrote Mr. Keeble years later. "The Lord had guided unmistakably and provided adequately. Praise His Name!" Once more He had proved that it is no vain thing to wait upon Him. "I cannot forbear mentioning the crowning miracle in those truly exciting days as we saw Him work for us who had waited for Him. We had £11,000 sterling to sell for our third quarter's needs. We purposely delayed selling till the very last moment, indeed till after the end of the previous quarter. Instead of cashing in at the pegged rate and obtaining $870,927 the British channel paid us $7,295,620. . . . The Lord's 'subsidy' being approximately 725 per cent!"

CHAPTER EIGHT

PLENTY OF SILVER

305 million dollars.
976 million dollars.
17,728 million dollars.

Such figures are startling. They represent the Mission's income in China for the years 1945, 1946 and 1947, and provide a graphic chart of what inflation means. For the stupendous sums of Chinese currency which were entered in the Mission ledgers, completely overrunning the columns provided, did not indicate a vast increase in income, but the rapid drop in the value of the Chinese dollar. It depreciated in value almost daily, until quarterly remittances for married couples ran into seven figures. In January, 1947 £1 sterling would purchase 13½ thousand National Chinese Currency dollars. By the end of the following year, £1 sterling would purchase 290 thousand Chinese National Currency dollars. A drop in value as drastic as from 20*s*. to a little less than 1*s*.!

The effect of inflation on the cost of living was devastating. Prices shot up over-night, so that a supply of money considered adequate for a month came to an end in a matter of days. On one occasion, when rates of exchange were adverse, the treasurer reported in a letter to the Home Director in England that a one lb. loaf of bread had cost the equivalent of 17*s*.! And a missionary in Kunming was informed by the British Consul there, whom he met in the street one day, that the cost of living was *seventeen* *times higher than it had been two months previously*. An index was carefully kept to observe this matter accurately. The official then continued his way. He was en route to the Telegraph Office to cable to London, announcing that it was impossible to continue living here in the present financial circumstances, and asking for instructions!

In 1948 an effort was made by the Nationalist Government to save the financial situation, and another currency was introduced, whereby *three million* of the old dollars would buy *one* new one! Before the end of the year, however, the new currency was going the way of the old. The only method whereby the Mission could conserve its finance was by keeping all money in sterling or U.S. dollars until the last possible moment, and then only exchanging sufficient for immediate needs. Yet even this method did not prove infallible. There was a time, just about VJ day, when the exchange dropped so unexpectedly and precipitately that the books showed a considerable loss on exchange. Normally, this would have caused some financial embarrassment. But it proved yet another of the innumerable occasions when those in the treasurer's department realized with thankfulness that Mission finance was in higher hands than theirs.

"To the glory of God be it stated that even this most unexpected and unprecedented strain did not embarrass our position in the least, so wonderful was the Lord's supply just at that time," ran the treasurer's report. One of the largest sums ever received in the London office up to that time had come to hand—the £15,000 mentioned in the Introduction.

Against such a background of economic instability and Divine security the Mission pursued its way through what proved to be its last half-decade in China. The unfailing remembrance of its material needs continued. As has so often been noted, when supplies from one source fell off, they increased from another. The accompanying chart demonstrates the way in which a balance was maintained between receipts from Great Britain and North America (U.S.A. and Canada), the areas from which more than two-thirds of Mission support is provided.

	1945	*1946*	*1947*	*1948*	*1949*	*1950*
U.S.$	203,910	232,090	168,000	152,000	252,000	284,000
£1	35,100	14,550	31,600	52,500	52,900	36,500

It will be observed that there is no drop in sterling contributions without there being a rise in U.S. dollar contributions and vice versa. In 1947, for instance, North American contributions were $64,000 less than in 1946—but Great Britain sent more than twice their total for the previous year. Yet even this chart reveals but inadequately the knowledge of Him who balances the clouds and hangs the world with perfect precision—on nothing! It reveals only the amount of money sent from North America and Great Britain. It does not take into account, for instance, the fact that in the years 1946 and 1947 missionaries were able to purchase at ridiculously low prices large supplies of surplus U.N.R.R.A. foodstuffs. Tins of peaches, cherries, asparagus, peas, coffee and boned chicken made little appeal to the masses of rice-eating Chinese; but when it was possible to obtain them at the rate of about 10*s.* for a 40-lb. case, they certainly eased the burdens of housekeepers in missionary establishments! Nor does the chart indicate that in 1950, when contributions from Great Britain to China fell by about one third, there was a substantial increase in those from Australia, South Africa, Switzerland and China, as well as from North America. It is also worthy of comment that while exchange rates for sterling were low, those for the U.S. dollar were relatively high. Like the little rivulets that trickle almost unnoticed into the stream to swell its waters, unexpected supplies and favourable rates of exchange time and time again helped to balance what appeared to be deficiencies in the Mission's income.

Let us now turn from the survey of statistics to more personal stories of God's provision for His children during those post-war years of economic and political chaos. For, after all, the financial position was accentuated by the political. "A kingdom divided against itself cannot stand," said One who sees to the heart of every human problem, national or individual. And China was in such a condition. The Communists in the north were advancing southwards and one after another, towns, cities and provinces were coming under their domination. For the missionaries living in those areas where there was fighting, it meant being cut off from Shanghai, the channel of their financial supplies, for weeks, perhaps months. Such a situation made the need for a supply of ready cash in a "safe" currency all the more acute.

Now there was, in the midst of all the flood of paper money that rapidly increased in quantity and decreased in quality in China at that time, a "safe" currency. People kept very quiet about it, and negotiated it in an undertone, for it was precious, difficult to obtain, and much coveted by officials. This "safe" currency was the silver dollar. Cast in a more stable age, the large round discs never lost their value, for it was intrinsic. One of them was worth hundreds, then thousands, then millions of paper dollars. Like a rock in the midst of a rushing stream, the silver dollar remained impregnable—though, also like the rock, almost entirely out of sight! Difficult indeed to come by was the silver dollar. But then, so had the gold bars in Shanghai been difficult to come by when the Japanese were in occupation.

"The silver is mine and the gold is mine, saith the Lord of hosts." Alien armies and seething political unrest cannot alter that fact one whit. What amazing confidence does this knowledge bring to those who trust in Him to supply their needs! Frank Parry and his colleagues obtained *gold* bars in 1941, and many are the stories that could be told of how the precious *silver* coins found their way into the possession of missionaries seven and eight years later. By ones and twos they were obtained usually, to be put aside for an emergency when ready money was needed in a hurry. But there was one remarkable occasion when silver dollars were obtained *by the wheelbarrow-load*!

It was in 1949, just before the collapse of the National Government. The Communists were crossing the Yangtze to invade the southern provinces, and Kiangsi was right in the line of their advance. In that province were not only about 100 C.I.M. missionaries, but nearly 200 children in the Mission's school on Kuling. How was sufficient money to be obtained to tide them all over the period of fighting? What money would still be negotiable, or have retained its value if and when the Communists were in control? The wealthy merchants who were glad to cash sterling or U.S. dollar cheques would certainly have departed! The national paper money would be worth less than half its present value within a few weeks. Shanghai headquarters would be cut off. Little wonder if Mr. Cyril Faulkner the superintendent and Mr. Walter Searle the local secretary spent many hours of many days going up and down the streets of Nanchang, searching for people who might be prepared to sell them a few silver dollars, and if an urgent request for silver daily found its way into their prayers and petitions to their almighty, but invisible Master. The Communist armies were drawing nearer and nearer, the wealthy were departing or going into hiding, and the store of the one safe currency was still wholly inadequate.

One morning, as the Faulkners were having morning prayers, Mrs. Faulkner suddenly said to her husband, "There you are. There's your promise!" He was rather surprised. They had come to the Book of Job in their daily readings, a book which is not, on the face of it, particularly plentiful in promises. In chapter 22 Eliphaz the Temanite hammers away on his contention that Job's affliction is the result of personal guilt. . . . Where is there any promise here for a man with the responsibility of providing safe currency for 300 people in the midst of civil war?

"Look at verse twenty-five again." He looked.

"Yea, the Almighty shall be thy defence, and thou shalt have *plenty of silver*."

"Plenty of silver!" Cyril Faulkner repeated the words wonderingly. Was it indeed God's personal assurance to him just now? Plenty of silver. It was strange that that phrase should have occurred just at this time of such dire need. It was just what they had been asking for—plenty of silver.

But on this particular day even silver was not his first concern. News had come that the Communist armies were advancing on the Kwangsin River area. In the towns along the banks of that river were a number of women missionaries, and they must be got out with all speed. "Yea, the Almighty shall be thy defence", was even more apt a promise to grasp at that moment! The superintendent departed for the Kwangsin River and extricated his fellow-workers just in time. After that he knew the fulfilment of the second half of the promise.

As he entered the compound yard, he saw a man standing there whom he had never met before.

"Are you Mr. Faulkner?" the stranger asked.

"Yes." 43218

"Are you wanting to buy silver?"

Yes, he was!

"Well, I can let you have some. . . ." The man was an oil merchant, preparing to flee from the Communists, and he wanted to travel light. In such circumstances, a cheque that would undoubtedly be honoured on arrival in Hongkong was exactly what he wanted. Such a cheque these missionaries, he knew, would give.

The following day Cyril Faulkner went to the merchant's office. Silver dollars were brought in in bundles, one after another, and emptied out until a pile of silver lay before him! Carefully the pieces were counted, tied up again, piled on a wheelbarrow and trundled unobtrusively round to the Mission premises. At last, and in the nick of time, there was plenty of silver!

There was still the problem of distributing it. The school was far away, and there were mission stations three and four days' journey from Nanchang to be supplied. Mr. Hayden Mellsop, a fellow missionary, undertook to get the school's supply through, and packing the coins in three ordinary-looking cardboard cartons, with the aid of a Bible School student, conveyed them through bandit-infested territory and up the steep mountainside to the school on Kuling. Then, as Cyril Faulkner was wondering whether he should take the money himself down to those other stations, and risk being cut off from his post in the capital, an acquaintance arrived in the city. He had come to collect a box of china and had travelled three days to do it! He was returning almost immediately—and his route took him through each one of those mission stations! Would he take the silver? Certainly he would. And so a bundle was deposited in each centre before the whole area was disrupted, and whatever other dangers and inconveniences the missionaries in Kiangsi

Lincoln Christian College

had to endure, at least they had plenty of silver!

Some time previously, in the far west of China, a little group of pioneer missionaries had been faced with an equally urgent need. The story of how the Gospel was taken right into independent Nosuland in the short period of time that elapsed between the end of the war in the Far East, and the withdrawal of missionaries from China, has been told by the leader of the team, Dr. A. J. Broomhall, in his book *Strong Man's Prey*. With his wife, four little children and two women colleagues he entered the territory of the barbarous, slave-raiding Nosu tribe. There a little mission house and a clinic were built—in the confidence that, although in this far-away place it would prove expensive, the project was of God.

When the building of the house and clinic started, only money sufficient for a month was in hand. But one of the advantages of not having a big bank balance in a work for God is the necessity it creates of walking close to Him. If the work is done at His direction, then certainly the provision will be His concern. If the project is merely human in conception, the sooner human resources fail the better. So the building in Nosuland was commenced and by the time more money was needed just sufficient came in. Sometimes all supplies had been used up before a new remittance arrived, but it always came in time. Then came a period when expenses mounted alarmingly—far beyond what they had anticipated, for even over on the borders of Nosuland the effects of inflation were being felt. The little group was faced with the realization that in a very short time some U.S.$900 would be needed to cover expenses. This was something bigger than they had reckoned on. No contributions made to the work had been anywhere near that sum. Picture the joy and delight of that little group, therefore, when on Dr. Broomhall's birthday, of all days, the sum of over U.S. $900 was received, as it were out of the blue—and more was to follow! The money came from England. It was a memorial fund to Anne Harcourt, a lady superintendent much loved and respected by the medical students whom she "mothered" and of whom Dr. Broomhall was one. Even if tangible evidence of God's guidance had been wanting before, this unexpected and perfectly timed contribution would have provided it; for it was as a medical student, in Miss Harcourt's "family" that Dr. Broomhall first heard of the independent Nosu amongst whom he was now working. "In those days it was only as a jest that we spoke of coming to Nosuland but even so the divinely planted whim was there." And now, nearly twenty years later, the pressing need was met from a fund inextricably connected with the days of that early call!

One more story must suffice to illustrate the intimate, personal manner of God's dealings with His people during that post-war period, and it comes, not from China itself, but from a journey to that country.

A missionary family, returning to China after the war, found themselves in Vancouver with no money. Owing to unforeseen delays and expenses, their travel allowance from England had proved insufficient. Their tickets for the train journey to San Francisco, and passages across the Pacific were paid, but they were faced with the long journey ahead, and no money at all in their pockets! They made their need known to no one but God, and set out.

On the way to the station they called at the home of relatives who had just said goodbye to a visitor who had left the house after giving $10 to his host for an unspecified object. The relative, knowing nothing of the need of the family, wondered if the $10 might not be for them! At the station another $5 note was given to one of them. That $15 was sufficient to provide them all with food for the two days' journey to San Francisco. Here they stayed in the home of Christian friends. It was a shock, however, to learn that a bill had been received from the shipping company for the transport of baggage from the docks to the boat. The bill amounted to nearly $20! But the first evening in San Francisco the father of the family was invited to speak at a small Bible School. Unknown to him a plate was left at the door and when the meeting was over the contents, which amounted to just under $20, were handed to him!

Eventually they boarded the liner, and set sail across the Pacific—penniless! Christmas was spent on board, and with four children it would have been embarrassing indeed to have no gifts and candies for them. But a friend in Buffalo had sent an order for a huge hamper to be delivered to them—including all manner of fruit, sweets and Christmas presents! No need for *them* to visit the ship's rather expensive shop, or to appear mean if they failed to do so!

Since it was a military transport, they concluded thankfully that there would be no tips to pay. But there were! The Passengers Organization decided that tips should be given at the rate of $1 per head—and even excluding the baby, that meant $5 for the family. Once more the need was made known only in secret—and the provision was made secretly too. An anonymous gift of $5 in an envelope was received on the very day the money for the tips was to be collected. It seemed there could be no more expenses and when on the following day they received another anonymous $5 there seemed no reason for it. But this time the need had been met ahead of time. One of the children went down with mumps, and this involved a tip to the nurse in the sick bay. Then they found that they would not be permitted to land unless their baby were innoculated—and this also required a fee. Both the expenses were met by that anonymous gift. When eventually the family reached Shanghai, they were as penniless as when they set out from Vancouver—but rich indeed in their experience of the God who has promised "And My people shall never be ashamed."

CHAPTER NINE

MULTIPLIED MONEY

MANY years ago, in the 'eighties, the secretary of the C.I.M. in London received a letter from a widow in Perth, enclosing 5*s*. She was, she explained, just on sixty, and apart from 2*s*. per week which was paid her by the parish, had no visible means of support. This fact, however, did not prevent her from sending money to two or three societies, among them the China Inland Mission, quite frequently. Only a little time previously she had sent 5*s*., and her chief reason for writing on this occasion was to tell of the Lord's goodness to her. Shortly after sending off that first costly gift, she had received a letter from someone who sent her 10*s*.! "The Lord is good. He never fails, praise His name. Sometimes I am in a strait, but He sends help." So now she wished to give half of it back to the Lord as a thank-offering!

Needless to say, Mr. Broomhall, deeply touched, replied promptly and warmly to this letter and a correspondence sprang up between him and the widow which lasted for twelve years, until the time of her death. She told no one else but him of the money which she sent for the work of God in China—money which, on the face of it, she simply could not afford. On one occasion, saddened by the reports of famine conditions in that country, she sent 8*s*. to the Mission, although, to quote her own words, "Satan said, 'Where will you get your 32*s*. for rent in May?' " (She did get it! A kind-hearted man to whom Mr. Broomhall told her story sent her the whole sum, forthwith!) One of her last conscious acts, as she lay on her lonely death-bed, was to send 5*s*. to Mr. Broomhall for the work in China. How she longed that her gifts, small in monetary value as they were, might somehow be multiplied. "I enclose for the C.I.M. postal order for 5*s*., and wish it were 5,000", she wrote once.

God has wonderful ways of answering such earnest desire and sacrifice. It is probable that the sum total of that widow's contributions over the years she was in touch with the Mission did not amount to more than £25. Yet on one occasion alone, in a single hour, that £25 was multiplied by 100. It is an interesting little story, illustrating as it does the fact that God is well able to increase mere monetary value.

Mr. Broomhall was invited to a breakfast party in the the West End home of a wealthy Christian man. Many interested questions were put to him about the work of the Mission and its support, and during the course of the conversation he drew from his pocket one of the widow's letters and read it aloud.

He can have been little prepared for the effect that letter would have on the hearers.

"It came to us as a shock to our personal indulgence, which put us to shame", wrote one afterwards. The host, a generous supporter of many Christian activities, exclaimed that all he had given had never involved him in the sacrifice of so much as one mutton chop! He had been in the habit of supporting home missions, rather than foreign ones, but now,

"I would like to give £500 to the China Inland Mission", he said. And turning to the man sitting next to him, he asked him what *he* would do! The outcome of that breakfast party, at which the widow's story was simply told and her letter read, was that £2,500 was contributed outright to the work for which she had prayed and sacrificed so whole-heartedly.

In writing of God's provision of material supplies, therefore, it is impossible to forbear reference to the small gifts that have been given at great personal sacrifice. We hear but few of the stories that lie behind the daily stream of unsolicited gifts from unknown friends, for those who give most sacrificially usually say least about it. It was only after some years, for instance, that the postal orders for 1*s.* 6*d.* which reached the London office of the Mission nearly every week were discovered to come from an old age pensioner who, when he went to draw his money, promptly sent off a small gift to the China Inland Mission. There was something sacramental in that act, performed as a weekly rite in a post office. The clerk behind the grille little knew that he was handling holy money as he passed over that 1*s.* 6*d.* postal order each week to the elderly man who came with the others, poor in this world's goods, to draw his pension. Not until the man's wife died, and he wrote to C.I.M. headquarters to ask that they would pray for him in his sorrow, did they know. But all through the years One who watches tenderly and lovingly over the sacrifices of His children had seen that weekly act—had He not been swift to answer the prayers of the unknown, godly old couple as they knelt before Him in their humble little home, to pray for the Mission to which their weekly offering went?

One day a missionary went to visit a lonely woman living in one room in a gloomy house in London. The sun never shone into that room, for it faced north, and very dull and dark it looked. During the course of the visit the woman asked the missionary to open her trunk and get out a little box containing a silver christening mug and spoon.

"It was my husband's", she explained. "I want you to sell it for me, and give the money to the Mission." The missionary was reluctant to agree. Would not that beautiful piece of silver, that held for the widow such sacred associations, look well on the mantelpiece? And if she really did not want to keep it, would she not use the money herself, to buy something she needed? But the woman was adamant. She had all she required. The Lord was very good to her, providing her with food and clothing. Her husband had wanted to go to China himself, as a young man. He would have been glad for the mug and spoon to be sold and the proceeds given to the Mission. So, one day, amongst the donations received was one for 25*s.*—the price of the weight of the silver. And the lonely woman in the room where the sun never shone was satisfied.

In Switzerland, the wife of the C.I.M. Secretary in that country became acquainted with an old lady who had been left practically penniless, and eked out a precarious living by doing knitting. In spite of her poverty, she gave small gifts to the Mission and then, one day, with a beaming face, she told her friend that the following week she would be sending some more money.

"You know my circumstances," she said. "It took me a long time to get the money together. But look at me. I am old, and it does not matter much what I eat. So, many times for dinner, I only take bread and water, in order to save money for the C.I.M., the Mission I feel I am called upon to pray for."

"It was only a few days later that the gift reached us," wrote Mrs. Baumann. "Fifty francs! Fifty holy francs. No—100 holy half-francs, perhaps 250 twenty-cent pieces, representing 250 times bread and water."

If human hearts are touched by such loving sacrifice, how much more must the tender heart of the Heavenly Father be moved at what He sees in secret? Will He not hearken to the prayers that accompany such "holy francs?" And will He not fulfil the earnest desire that those small gifts may in some way be multiplied to meet the needs?

Perhaps it was in answer to some such prayers, accompanying similarly holy money, that two missionaries with broken health were led in 1928 to stay in a little cottage that had been lent to them in the country. It so happened that this cottage was adjacent to a large estate belonging to a wealthy Christian lady who, although she had not known them previously, in various little ways befriended them. When, later, a C.I.M. meeting was to be held in a neighbouring town she expressed regret that she would not be free on that day, but went on to say that she would very much like to give something for the collection. They thanked her, but explained that in accordance with C.I.M. practice, there would not be a collection!

"Well," she replied, "is there not some special need in the Mission just now, where I could help?"

As they both knew, there *was* a need. It was one about which they, with others, had recently prayed. The front buildings of the London headquarters were in a somewhat dilapidated condition. For a long time it had been recognized that to remain habitable they would need extensive and expensive repairs, and were actually so inconvenient that such money would be but badly invested. The Mission leaders therefore prayed earnestly that special funds for more suitable buildings might be made available. Meanwhile the front premises at Newington Green continued to deteriorate; and to make matters worse, had recently been condemned by the authorities.

When, therefore, the two missionaries were asked the direct question, "Is there not some special need in the Mission just now?" they could not but answer in the affirmative. There was in fact this particular need for rebuilding at headquarters. . . .

"How much would be required for such a building?"

They knew the approximate sum, for tentative plans

had been drawn and estimates made, although there was no apparent possibility of commencing work for years to come. Somewhat reluctantly they answered,

"About £20,000."

"Well," came the unexpected reply, "couldn't I do that? Couldn't I just give those buildings?"

Give them she did—and their furnishings.[1] They stand to-day, the hostel for candidates, flats for staff members and flatlets for retired missionaries, simple yet dignified, with a front on which are displayed, for all to see, the words, "Have faith in God". They stood throughout the blitz, when all around buildings were being destroyed by enemy bombs. On one occasion ten houses a few yards away were burnt out—and about twenty people in them lost their lives. But the C.I.M. compound was almost unscathed. On another night a 1,000-lb. bomb dropped right through the roof of an adjoining building without exploding and lay unnoticed for several days. But it was discovered in time. The area was cordoned off, and the bomb safely removed. "The C.I.M. is the safe place," the Air Raid Precaution staff who were billetted in those front buildings were heard to exclaim. And the A.R.P. men were so impressed by the deliverance that they came with the request, most gladly granted, that a service of thanksgiving be held in the C.I.M. Prayer Hall. Of all the buildings in the vicinity, the C.I.M. front building alone escaped the bombings virtually unharmed—although there was a window in one of the top floor flatlets, through which a piece of shrapnel whizzed, making a hole the size of a marble!

Such large gifts as £20,000 are, of course, received but rarely, and usually come in the form of legacies. In days gone by, there have sometimes been very considerable

[1] A further £8,000 was received later from this friend for the same object.

additions to the Mission's income through the Lord's servants who, when setting their house in order, have allotted a proportion of their earthly treasure to be given for the work of extending God's kingdom in the Far East. Of recent years, however, heavy taxation and death duties in England have made such inroads into the estates of the erstwhile well-to-do, that legacies are of necessity much smaller comparatively. This fact makes the legacy that was received in the London offices early in 1955 all the more remarkable.

Perhaps it should be explained that while the money received on the field is distributed equally to members of the Mission there, irrespective of what country they come from, each home centre is responsible for its own upkeep. Retired missionaries, missionaries on furlough, members of the home staff, are supplied from the headquarters of their own home country. In addition, it is always the aim of each home centre to send to the field sufficient to support the workers who have gone forth from it. When this aim is unrealized over a long period, it results in much exercise of heart. As month after month went by in 1954, therefore, and the income received at Newington Green was consistently below that which was normally required, those responsible for the disbursement of funds were conscious anew of their dependence upon the Lord. Quietly another little weekly prayer meeting, to be held each Tuesday, was commenced in the Mission Home—a private prayer meeting, to pray especially about the matter of funds. Only members of the Mission and colleagues on the office staff were expected to attend, for only to the Father in heaven was the matter to be revealed. Lest public prayer for an increased income should be interpreted as an indirect appeal to man, the subject was not referred to at all at open meetings. It was, however, mentioned frequently and urgently in private, accompanied by personal soul-searching to ensure that no Achan-like sin was withholding blessing from the whole body.

The year 1954 closed with all accounts paid, but with very little balance in hand—and with some further lessons learnt in the art of economy! During December a bequest of £1,836 which it had seemed was to come to the Mission, went instead to a Bible School organized by Chinese in the Far East. The money was left by a wealthy lady in America, and the terms of the will regarding the sum being so interpreted, the money was duly passed on. What happened after that can best be described by a private letter written by the Rev. G. A. Scott, now Home Director in Great Britain.

"We were glad for our Chinese friends, for the amount would mean much to them," he observed. "As for our own needs, they were known to God, and we reminded ourselves, 'He is able to give thee much more than this.' But we were totally unprepared for the literal fulfilment of this promise when a further communication from the same source a few days later advised us of an amount being sent *to the Mission* which proved to be—£25,000!"

£25,000![1] Little wonder that the Doxology was sung at that small, private prayer meeting on the very next Tuesday! "The Lord is able to give thee much more than this", had been the promise on which confidence had rested at the time when the £1,700 that seemed so sorely needed, was passed on. "Much more than this. . . ." Just about fifteen times as much, on this occasion!

The remarkable thing about this particular legacy is its source. It came from the U.S.A., the will being that of an American lady whom nobody in C.I.M. appeared to know at all! How she became interested in the Mission is

[1] A further sum of nearly £20,000 was later received from this same estate.

a mystery. In 1944 she sent a small donation to the London office, and one in each of the three years following. Then nothing further was heard from her until 1950, when another comparatively small donation was received. From that time on she had no correspondence with the Mission. Since she lived in America, it would have been the most natural thing for her to have left her money to the C.I.M. in that country—instead, it was given to the headquarters in the United Kingdom. The explanation that comes most readily to mind is that her only contact with the Mission was through reading something published in England, and that she did not even know of its existence in her own country. Whatever the reason, the money came at a time of financial straitness for the home centre in England, while that in North America was enjoying a period of some plenty. So God meets the needs of those who trust in Him. Like the Israelites of old, "he that gathered much had nothing over, and he that gathered little had no lack". And the very unexpectedness of the channels He uses helps to ensure that we look only unto Him.

CHAPTER TEN

THE WITHDRAWAL

IT was 1951, the year of the withdrawal. As long as the Mission lasts, this year will be remembered. In all the ninety years of its history no year has been so sad, so poignant, and so abundant in mercy and grace. The sadness of drawing out of China; the possibilities in the hitherto unknown lands of Southeast Asia; the perplexity, the sense of stepping out on to thin air, the anxiety about missionaries who were unable to obtain exit visas; encircling all the experiences and emotions contained in this memorable year was the unfailing goodness of God, manifested in an unusual measure in material supplies. For in this year, with its unprecedented expenses and alarming bills, there was always plenty to meet every demand. Not just sufficient—plenty. Whatever might be the heart-aches, the disappointments, the strains and the tensions of leaving China and starting from scratch in strange lands, a sense of financial stringency was never allowed to intensify them. "He stayeth His rough wind in the day of the east wind."

And yet, when the fateful decision was taken, how formidable seemed the prospect. For it was estimated that, apart from normal overhead expenses, it would cost over £100,000[1] to withdraw the Mission personnel from China. That figure in itself was a sufficient deterrent to a hasty decision! Little wonder that when, from various sources, questions were asked about the wisdom of remaining in China, there was always one good answer.

[1] The actual figure was about £113,000.

"The Lord sets His seal on our staying at least in this one indication, that He has not given us the wherewithal to withdraw", was written in a private letter from Shanghai in September, 1950. "It is interesting that since the troubles increased, we have received only one gift specially earmarked 'For evacuation, if such be the Mission's policy.' It was a gift of U.S.$1,000. But not another penny."

If there were few financial indications apart from that significant U.S.$1,000 that the time had come to leave China, however, there were not lacking indications of another kind. From all over China were coming reports of increasing restrictions on the liberty of missionaries. A number were confined to their compounds, and a few were actually imprisoned. Furthermore, the witness to Christ was being silenced as the stigma of being agents to the "Imperialist nations" was attached to those who were even remotely associated with missionaries. It was this crippling suspicion attaching to Chinese Christians that was the main factor in the decision to withdraw.

On the more practical side, there was one rather interesting little indication that the Lord was beginning to remove His missionary servants which did not altogether escape the observation of those in administrative positions. In the year 1950 an unusually large number of people had to leave the country for health reasons. One after another, it seemed, workers were being invalided home. As early as May, attention was drawn to it in a letter from Hongkong. "It is interesting to notice how many are having to leave China these days because of ill-health. I wonder if you have thought why the Lord is using this means of thinning our numbers." Six months later, in a letter from headquarters in Shanghai, the matter is referred to in a comment on a donation earmarked in a somewhat unusual way. It was the sum of

£200 for passage money for those who needed to return home for health reasons. "These friends have obviously sensed what we have felt so keenly, namely the number of our workers who of late have had to go home for health reasons. Possibly it is the way the Lord is using to slim down our numbers in view of the situation."

Nevertheless, even in November, Mission policy was still to remain in China. Somewhat reluctantly a new ruling permitted those who wished to leave the country to do so while still retaining membership in the Mission, but they must travel at their own expense. The thought of leaving China altogether, deserting their Chinese brethren in the hour of their distress, could not be entertained. The undeniable fact was, however, that the hour of distress was not alleviated but intensified by this well-meaning loyalty. November days came and went, bringing more and more reports of Chinese church leaders who, with what measure of frankness their innate courtesy and Christian love would allow, said that things would really be easier for them if the Western missionaries departed. Some even begged them to do so. So at last, after staff meetings, expressions of opinion, the weighing of evidence and the consideration of the Lord's "indications", in mid-December it was agreed that the time had come. The entire Mission must prepare to withdraw.

There is a strange similarity between the Mission's early beginnings, when the first party was preparing to sail to China, and this period when it was preparing to leave. The Mission was born of a deep conviction that it was God's will—and with a bank account of £10! Twenty-four workers were asked for as a beginning, and the estimated cost of sending out the first large party was between £1,500 and £2,000. In the beginning of February 1866, only £170 was in hand, and the party was to sail in

May. But the conviction of God's will was so strong that plans and confident prayers were quietly and simultaneously made, with the result that in May the whole party boarded the *Lammermuir* with all expenses met and a substantial sum in hand.

In December, 1950, that same deep conviction of God's will caused the launching of the withdrawal—a project requiring £113,000 for travelling expenses, when only £1,500 was on the Passages Account.[1]

When 1951 opened, a balance of £11,600 was entered from the previous year—approximately 10 per cent. of the money required, much the same proportion as was in hand for the sailing of the *Lammermuir* party eighty-five years previously.

"We have now granted leave of departure for a large number of people for whom we are unable to make any provision for their passages out of Hongkong," wrote the Mission treasurer in Shanghai on December 27th. "We are all much in prayer that the Lord will do some big thing. . . . He is able."

It was seen later how able He was. But in those early days, it was a case of hoping for that which was not yet seen. The step had been taken, from which there was no turning back, and the withdrawal was under way. Missionaries were beginning to travel down to Hongkong from all over China to await shipping to take them back to their home countries; passages were few and far between; and the cost of living in Hongkong was the highest on the whole of the Mission's list of centres! "By far the heaviest cost of maintenance is for our friends in Hongkong," the treasurer had written home a few months earlier. "This is a most expensive place." And

[1] In normal times 5 per cent. of the Mission's income on the field is placed in the Passages Account to meet the need of missionaries leaving for furlough.

now the whole of the Mission would be crossing the border into the beautiful Crown Colony with every prospect of being held up there for months before passages home could be procured! Little wonder if one letter written at that time ended with the words, "These are grim days. We are counting much on your prayers." But another voiced the quiet confidence felt by all who were bearing the responsibility. "Financially, the whole situation is just staggering, but we have a strong faith by the grace of God that He alone will do wondrous things for us."

We will now contemplate some of those wondrous works, and to do so, let us first picture an attractive little flat on the water front in Kowloon, where lived the two C.I.M. families who were actually stationed in Hongkong. The news had just been received that the entire personnel of the Mission was to evacuate from China, and would be converging on Hongkong, where they must, of course, be housed until passages could be obtained for them to return home! And Mr. and Mrs. Ament looked at each other, made rapid mental household re-arrangements, and realized that even by cramming their three small boys into one single bedroom, and sleeping themselves in the office, they could really not accommodate more than about half a dozen people at a time. That meant, of course, so long as the people had not much baggage! And shortly there would be a stream of several hundreds of men, women and children descending on them, complete with what personal belongings they had been able to bring! Something must be done, and done quickly.

How best to describe the ceaseless activity of the days that followed? First lists must be made of all the C.I.M. missionaries and children and presented to the police and immigration authorities. Refugees from China were pouring into the overcrowded Colony by their thousands, and were already creating grave problems. Mr. Ament must guarantee that these people for whom he would be responsible should pass through the Colony with the minimum of delay. He visited shipping offices to reserve what tourist class passages were available to the home countries—far, far too few to begin to meet the need! But over and above these requirements was the immediate and urgent need for accommodation.

There was no accommodation available. Visits to hotels and house agents all over Hongkong evoked little more than helpless shrugs and expressions of regret. During the past two years the estimated population of Hongkong had increased from one million to two and a half. The poorer Chinese refugees were sleeping in the streets or in the hovels they had made out of boxes, cardboard, sacking, anything they could obtain; the wealthy ones were paying as much as 50,000 Hongkong dollars "key money" and a monthly rent of 2,000 for a house. For one room in a tenement 5,000 Hongkong dollars "key money" was being demanded—and obtained! One small hotel, run by Chinese Christians, promised accommodation for a few missionaries at a reduced rate, and that was about all! At one stage there seemed the possibility of renting a Chinese school building which would house about 250 people, but the military obtained possession of it first, and nothing else presented itself.

Eventually Mr. Ament went to see a very highly placed official in the Colony. He, surely, could provide some solution! But although he was extremely sympathetic he had no suggestion to offer. Even top-level officials could not produce empty buildings in Hongkong in those days. "I'll see what I can do," was the kind assurance, but very little hope was held out that he could do anything. "Keep in touch, and let me know if you get anything." And then came the news that the children from the schools in Kuling were to be evacuated almost immediately, and the first large party would be arriving in a week's time!

The ceaseless round of visits to likely and unlikely people and places continued—and the ceaseless, earnest prayer to the One who long ago pointed out that foxes have holes, and birds have nests. . . . Surely the God who had never failed to hear His children's cry would not be silent now! So in the confidence that the Lord of Hosts was with him, Mr. Ament went on working at the seemingly impossible task of obtaining accommodation. Somewhere that accommodation was waiting, and if he went on seeking, he would surely find it.

He had no particular presentiment that he was just on the point of finding it when he decided to pay one more visit to an estate agent to whom he had already applied many times before. How often God leads His servants when they have no consciousness that it is so. The obvious, normal round of duty presents itself, and as they proceed therein they suddenly find themselves confronted with some Divine commission or plan of which they had not dreamed. It was so now. As he entered the office, the estate agent glanced at him keenly, and then said,

"Take a seat. You look as though you've had it!" and as Mr. Ament sank gratefully into the proffered seat, he added ruefully, "And I'm afraid my news won't help you. I just can't find you anything."

The two men looked at each other, and the estate agent, eager to help yet conscious of his inability to do so, continued,

"What you need is a dozen Nissen huts. You could fix them up, and make them quite habitable."

"Yes, I'd thought of that," came the reply. "I've even been to the top level, to see if they know of any. They tell me there is not one available in the Colony."

Nissen huts . . . empty Nissen huts. . . .

The estate agent stared at Mr. Ament, unseeing. In the dim recesses of his memory something was stirring—something he had seen, which at the time had made no impression, but now . . .

Suddenly he sat bolt upright in his chair.

"I know where there are eleven empty Nissen huts," he announced.

Bob Ament sat up, too!

"Where?" he demanded.

"Chatham Road."

The missionary's hopes subsided immediately. He lent back in his chair again and shook his head.

"Listen," he said, "I live right along there, in Chatham Road, and I know those huts. They are practically opposite our flat. They are all occupied by the military."

"I know," replied the house agent. "But I was there a month ago, and on a separate block of land, beyond that receiving end of the crematorium, there are eleven, and they are empty." He described their position, and then said, "Go and see if they are still vacant."

Mr. Ament needed no second bidding. Across the harbour he went, back along the familiar stretch of Chatham Road to where it crossed the railway siding. There he turned down a private road by the railway track that led to the water-front. Sure enough, out of sight of the road stood eleven Nissen huts. Deserted-looking, dilapidated, in poor condition certainly—but they were empty!

All physical weariness was forgotten in the jubilant hope that this was the solution to the problem. Back across the ferry went Mr. Ament, this time to see, not the estate agent, but the high-ranking official. Those Nissen huts were Government property. And when the Government servant heard of them, he said, "Well, I didn't know of these! Now we've got to go through *three*

Government departments—and I suppose you've heard of red tape?"

"Yes," was the reply, "And in less than a week now the first large party is due to arrive."

The two men sat silent. Red tape. Files. Restrictions. Agreements. Bye-laws. A crowd of British and American schoolchildren were coming down out of Communist China into Hongkong, and there was nowhere for them to stay!

The high-ranking official did not know any of those children personally. Neither did the heads of those three Government departments. But the kinship of nations is, after all, very strong, and Government departments are manned with human beings, not robots. Would any of them be likely to untie "red tape" so slowly as to fail to meet the needs of those children?

"Listen," he said, "I'm so sure you'll get those huts that I'll take the risk of telling you to go ahead and make them habitable!"

There was not a minute to be wasted now. The huts were actually in the process of being demolished, and all water-piping and electrical installations had already been removed. Unless demolition work were ceased immediately and the place put into repair, there would still be no place for that party, complete with baggage, when they arrived. Indeed, with so short a time left and so much to be done, it still seemed impossible that they could be ready in time.

The fact that they were ready in time is due to another of God's provisions—not of a fund of money, but something of far greater value—a Christian friend. This Christian friend was the member of a well-known Hongkong family, and one who had already shown himself deeply concerned over the matter of obtaining accommodation for the evacuating missionaries. It was to this architect and engineer that Mr. Ament turned now.

He was scarcely less delighted and relieved than Mr. Ament himself at the discovery of the huts. Water needed to be laid on? He contacted the Waterworks office. Beds and bedding required? He got in touch with the Social Welfare Officer. Insufficient wiring and fittings obtainable for the electrical installations? He had a quantity which for some reason he had refused to sell, even when the demand for it was sending the prices high. It should be used now. No authority to erect poles for overhead cables on railway property? He obtained permission from the Manager of Railways. Personal and business concerns were put completely aside, it seemed, as he and his staff worked and organized to get those derelict huts in a habitable condition to receive the parties travelling down through China. Nor did his interest cease when he saw the children comfortably and happily settled in those long huts with their rows of beds. He had children of his own. Showers and wash basins were installed in the camp—but no baths. So day after day the architect and his wife drove up to take a car-load of children to their own beautiful home, where they were given the freedom of the bathrooms!

How inadequate, after all, are Mission accounts. So much money received—so much money expended. Money is but a fraction of our Heavenly Father's provision. Service freely rendered, open homes and open hearts—these things cannot be entered up under pounds, shillings and pence. Records kept in heaven are much more detailed, where even so much as a cup of cold water is noted—for the future fulfilment of the promised reward.

The provision of that group of huts, so aptly dubbed "Freehaven" was one of the wondrous doings of God during the withdrawal year. It is no exaggeration to say that it saved the Mission thousands of pounds. Through the good services of another friend an excellent caterer was found, who cooked and served meals on the camp itself. The whole problem of accommodation in Hongkong was solved outright.

There still remained the question of how to get the evacuated missionaries to their home countries, however, and at the commencement of the year it looked as though even Freehaven, with its accommodation for as many as 180 people at a time, would be inadequate. Hongkong threatened to become a bottleneck with large parties arriving, and then departing in ones and twos whenever sea passages could be obtained. Visits and telephone calls were made to all the shipping offices almost daily, but the waiting lists were so long already that it was evident it would be months before people could get away from Hongkong. Apart from the expense involved in keeping them there was the even more important consideration of delaying them from proceeding to the new fields which were already opening up. The sooner they gained the spiritual and physical renewal which furlough is intended to provide, the sooner would they be back again on the mission-fields of Southeast Asia. Furthermore, assurance had been given to the immigration authorities that those coming into Hongkong from China would move on immediately, and failure to fulfil this condition might well cause difficulty with the Government. From every point of view it seemed urgent that a quick way out of Hongkong be found.

After every avenue had been explored, however, it seemed that there was no such way other than by using the costly air routes, or the expensive saloon classes on liners. Once again it was a case of looking to the Lord, praying that He would provide the swift transport which seemed quite unobtainable—and continuing to seek, in spite of the apparent uselessness of doing so. None of the shipping agents in the Colony were left in any uncertainty as to the fact that the C.I.M. required passages to the homelands!

One day the manager of Thomas Cook's Travel Agency inquired whether the C.I.M. would be interested in chartering planes to London. The reply was not encouraging. This possibility had already been explored, it was explained, and would prove far too expensive. But the manager of Cook's continued,

"I've heard of some chartered planes going to Japan with freight, and returning to London empty. Maybe something could be arranged with them."

This sounded more hopeful, and the next time one of these planes landed in Hongkong, the pilot was approached. Was there any possibility of him taking a freight-load of human passengers on his return flight?

Indeed there was, the pilot replied! Various attempts had been made by the company to obtain payloads for the return journeys to London—but in vain. Every door had been closed, and the planes were flying home empty. It is "He that shutteth, and no man openeth," who promises, "Knock, and it shall be opened to you." Were not those doors closed in order that this one might be opened to His people who were praying for swift transport?

After that first inquiry, arrangements were made quickly. The price of flying people home on those planes, it was discovered, would be but a fraction higher than the fare charged in the P. and O. liner tourist class! And so, over a period of about four months seven or eight plane-loads of thirty to forty people took off from Hongkong airfield, en route for London, carried on Eagles wings literally, for that was the name of the airline!

How accurately are our needs known to God! At the commencement of that four months it seemed that at least ten or eleven chartered planes would be necessary.

But people were not getting out of China as quickly as had been expected. Exit visas were not granted as readily as had been hoped. The time came when the C.I.M. representative realized that he had not sufficient passengers to fill the next plane he had booked. Arrangements had already been made, however, and could scarcely be altered now. It seemed that this trip would prove an expensive one.

Two days before the plane was due to take off, Mr. Ament went to the agent to hand in the list of passengers—a very short list, this time. The agent was apologetic.

"I'm sorry," he said. "The flight is off. We have just had word that the plane cannot re-fuel in India, because of the troubles in Abadan." Just at the time when the need ceased to exist, the provision was withdrawn!

It was during one of those flights home that the passengers had a vivid reminder of the word spoken thousands of years ago, "I do set My bow in the cloud". After three days, when visibility had been particularly good, on the fourth and last day the plane flew into mist and cloud. No longer could the earth be seen; but suddenly, looking out of the window, one of the travellers stiffened as she gazed, transfixed, on the clouds below. For there she saw a rainbow. It was not, however, as the rainbow is often seen from the earth, a beautiful arc stretching from horizon to horizon. This rainbow was no arc, but a complete circle, unbroken, perfect. Nor was that all. In the very centre of the rainbow, like the apple of an eye, was a shadow. It was the shadow of the plane in which they were travelling. As the shadow sped across the clouds, so that colourful, luminous circle, like a shining protection surrounding it, sped too. Never was the shadow anywhere but in the very centre of the rainbow. What clear skies could not reveal was shown in the clouds. How often is it so! The reassuring consciousness of God's presence is rarely known to the same degree in the sunshine as in the storm. It is in the cloud that He sets His bow.

It was so in the clouds of the withdrawal. As each new emergency arose, so came fresh evidence of His faithfulness who has promised, "I will never leave thee, nor forsake thee". The provision of Freehaven, the transport planes, the £28,000 from the renting of the Shanghai property referred to in the first chapter, these were the more spectacular evidences of His care and power. They were not the only ones. The first tangible token for good came in the shape of a special gift amounting to £3,775 from American headquarters immediately after the news had been received of the decision to withdraw. Throughout the period of January to November, 1951, £32,000 was received, specially earmarked for passages, over and above the remittances from the homelands to General Funds which were well in advance of normal requirements. A particularly touching gift was a generous donation towards travelling expenses received from some Chinese Christians. Another source of income for the emergencies of this year was the funds which had been set aside for projects in China which could not now be fulfilled. While it has never been Mission policy to put aside money "for a rainy day" it has always been its policy to make preparations for advance. The unfinished task has always been too great and too apparent to be forfotten in the necessary work of consolidation. After survey and prayer, plans to go forward in one or several directions are decided on, and special accounts opened to finance them. For instance, it had been planned to erect hospital buildings in West Yunnan, and about £10,000 had already been drafted, during past months, from General Funds to this account. It would obviously be useless to commence that building now, so the money was drafted back into General Funds, where it was made available for passages, or whatever need arose. Although this was the largest of the "special" accounts, there were a number of smaller ones which amounted to over £15,000. It is interesting to note, however, what happened to money that had been sent by donors for a specific purpose for which it could not now be used. Several letters were sent from the treasurer in Shanghai to the treasurer in London, containing lists of names with varying sums of money alongside them, some of less than £1, asking him to get in touch with donors to find out whether, in the circumstances, they now wanted the money back, or used for other purposes. There seems to be no record of donors having asked for their money back!

So the year rolled on. "We are not being embarrassed at all for cash," wrote the treasurer in May. "Indeed, we are over-stocked at the moment!"

"The balance of U.S.$89,325 on Passages Account indicates that we now have in hand sufficient for about 225 more passages," he wrote in July.

"We have experienced no straitness of any kind," he reported in October. And when he wrote his annual financial letter to Home Directors he commenced,

"In thinking over the events of 1951, there is only one word which, constantly returning to my mind, adequately described the Lord's provision for so cataclysmic a year, and that is that generous word PLENTY which surely is entirely characteristic of our God. Joel chapter 2, verse 26 stands out:

"And ye shall eat in plenty and be satisfied, and praise the name of the Lord your God, that hath dealt wondrously with you; and my people shall never be ashamed."

Briefly, January, 1951 opened with £11,600 in hand and almost the whole Mission to evacuate. By November all but about twenty were safely out, and a sum of £10,500 on the right side indicated there was sufficient to meet their needs for passages when they emerged! During the year about U.S. $84,000 had been withdrawn from the "Special Accounts" for forward movement projects in China to the General Fund. But as the year advanced, the still larger sum of U.S. $93,000 was transferred from General Fund to "Special Accounts"—mainly for advance into the new fields of Southeast Asia.

It was with a full heart that the treasurer concluded his report for the year with the words,

"I cannot but add to our heartfelt praises to an Almighty God, our unstinted gratitude to all the donors in the homelands who so magnificently by prayer and gift saw the Withdrawal through."

How good is the God we adore,
Our faithful, unchangeable Friend,
Whose love is as great as His power
And knows neither measure nor end.

'Tis Jesus, the first and the last,
Whose Spirit shall guide us safe Home,
We'll praise Him for all that is past,
And trust Him for all that's to come.

CHAPTER ELEVEN

PLACES TO LIVE IN

"AND trust Him for all that's to come."

That Abraham left Ur of the Chaldees to go to the land of Canaan as the result of a direct revelation and command from God, the Bible makes quite clear. The Lord appeared to him, and under that divine compulsion he went forth, not knowing whither. What is not made evident, however, is the manner in which he was led to the land of promise. Is it unreasonable to suppose that his steps and his stops were largely determined by such practical considerations as the position of water and pasture for his herds? That many a time he gathered up his tent and moved a little further west, a few degrees to the north, or fetched a compass to the south, not as the outcome of a dream or vision in the night, but simply because a servant found a well, or reported good grazing land a distance away?

The life of faith in this world is lived in the midst of economic and material necessity, and many times it is through the supply or denial of practical and mundane requirements that guidance is given. The story of how the decision was made by Mission leaders to take up work in Japan is a case in point.

It was early in 1951 that the Home Directors from North America, Great Britain, Australia, New Zealand and South Africa, together with the General Director and a China Director met in Australia to seek God's face regarding the future of the Mission. The withdrawal was already under way, and there was no time to lose. Some of the men who attended that conference had cancelled all their engagements and travelled half way round the world in order to be there. Two days were spent in prayer before meetings for discussion were commenced, and by the third day of the conference all were agreed that steps should be taken towards establishing missionaries in most of the countries in Southeast Asia. There was, however, one country about which there was a large measure of doubt in the minds of those men who were united in their desire to know and to do the will of God. One country had been suggested which was beyond the orbit of the region known as Southeast Asia. Did God's plan for the C.I.M. extend as far as Japan?

At the dawning of the day in which the matter was to be decided, therefore, no one could foretell what would be the result of the discussion. There was quite as much reason to expect that the decision would be against entering Japan as that it would be for it. And then something happened which turned the scales. In the morning mail that was delivered in that rather remote spot were two letters both bearing upon Japan. One was from the director of a missionary society at work in Africa. He had himself made a survey of Japan, and was deeply impressed by its spiritual needs. The sum of U.S.$1,000 had been given him for the opening of work there, but his mission finally decided that it could not embark on this new project. What, then, was to be done with the money specifically contributed for this purpose? Hearing of the possibility of C.I.M. opening work in other countries in East Asia, he wrote to say that should they decide to enter Japan, the $1,000 would be made available to them. The other letter was from quite a different source, and contained a donation for £500—but with the suggestion that half of it be used to explore the possibilities of commencing work in—Japan.

These two gifts from men of God, arriving on the very

day when Japan was the main subject for discussion, provided a tangible form of guidance which left little doubt in anyone's mind as to the Lord's will on the subject. Japan was included in the Mission's new outreach, and in various ways the step taken then has been confirmed since. Little churches being established, souls being saved, the Gospel being preached where before it was not heard, are the evidences of His blessing. But for the perfect timing of those two letters, however, the entry into Japan might well have been delayed for months—not so much because of lack of means, as because of lack of assurance. God's stewards rendered a double service when they sent their gifts *at the right time*.

Perhaps in no way more than in the provision of places to live in, however, has His hand been revealed in the entry into the new fields. For when it was decided that work be undertaken in Thailand, Malaya, Indonesia, Philippines, Formosa and Japan, with headquarters in Singapore, the Mission possessed not so much as a foot of land in any of these places, let alone any premises. And in almost every country in the Far East, they were warned, the housing shortage was such that it was extremely difficult to buy suitable houses, and just about impossible to rent them.

Now it had early been agreed that the Mission should *not* purchase property, in the lands to which it was now going, as it had in China. This decision was not made arbitrarily, but for a very sound reason, and it was made after much prayer and consideration. There was an ever deepening conviction that converts in these new fields must from the very outset learn to depend on God, who gives His Spirit to all who trust His Son, and not to depend on the missionary. "The time is short." There was an eleventh hour sense of urgency about this entry into South-east Asia and Japan. No one believed that even those doors would remain open very long. China, wherein dwelt nearly a quarter of the world's population, was closed already, and the uprise of nationalism in the newly awakened countries of the East, together with the evident spread of Communism, boded ill for Western missionary enterprise. Ere long it seemed most, if not all, of the countries in the Far East must be left, and if converts there were not spiritually hardy, with a developed faith that relies on God alone, how would they be able to stand? Hot-house methods are fruitless if gardeners have to depart—seeds have a better chance sown in the open ground! Therefore it was decreed that no places of meeting would be provided by the Mission for little groups of converts, however poor. And that missionaries should wherever possible live in hired houses, from which they could move promptly if necessity arose, or if they were required elsewhere. As a matter of policy the Mission would not buy.

The policy was sound, both from the practical as well as the spiritual point of view. The question was—could houses for moderate rents be obtained in countries where the Mission was unknown, where the missionaries knew not the language of the people with whom they must negotiate, and where the housing shortage was acute? It seemed impossible. And it is in apparently impossible situations that faith is called into action. "The province of faith begins where probabilities cease and sight and sense fail," affirmed George Muller, that giant of faith of the last century. "Faith has nothing to do with probabilities." On that point, at any rate, the policy to rent rather than buy was sound—for on the human level it just would not work!

It is interesting to notice that when Mr. Percy Moore first went to Singapore, early in 1952, in order to find premises for the Mission's headquarters, which were still operating in Hongkong, the plan was for him to look for property for sale. The prohibition on purchasing houses does not apply to buildings to be used for the administration of Mission affairs. He looked in vain. He went up and down the streets, lanes, roads and footpaths of the island day after day, and found nothing, returning wearily at evening to the home in New Bridge Road where he was staying. It was at this very house, then the property of the London Missionary Society, that Hudson Taylor arranged for C.I.M. workers to stay when they had to tranship for China, during the last century! But one day a telegram arrived from Hongkong. The Mission leaders there had just had a meeting, and suggested that as efforts to buy premises had failed, it might be the Lord's will for premises to be rented.

"As soon as I received this telegram I thought to myself how much harder it was to rent than to buy under the present conditions existing here, and that it would be almost impossible to rent such a big place as we would need," wrote Mr. Moore. Nevertheless he set about attempting what seemed impossible, and within two hours of receiving the telegram he was three miles from the city, looking over a twenty-roomed boarding house that was—to let! The rent demanded was quite reasonable. Furthermore, the place was fully equipped and the occupants wanted to sell all the furniture outright and were of course, therefore prepared to let it go cheap! The whole problem of house-hunting was solved outright, and that of furnishing did not even arise. In less than three months 33 Chancery Lane, Singapore 11 was established as the headquarters of the C.I.M. Overseas Missionary Fellowship.

The next big step came in 1954, when it was quite evident that further accommodation would be required. New recruits from the homelands were pouring in in a steady stream, and a permanent language school was needed to provide them all with a preliminary course of study before proceeding to their destinations. The Chancery Lane building, therefore, should become the language school as soon as other premises were provided for the headquarters staff. So once again inquiries were set on foot to discover where suitable land for building could be obtained at a reasonable figure. Eventually very suitable land was located—but not at a figure which the Mission could afford.

It was a very suitable site, that plot on Cluny Road. In addition to the seven bedroomed house, ideal for a mission home with its large, airy living-room, there was plenty of land on which to build the necessary offices and flats for the headquarters staff. Gifts were already coming in, especially earmarked for new buildings in Singapore. But when tentative inquiries were made, it was discovered that the price asked for that plot of ground was 170,000 Malay dollars, more than twice as much as the Mission had in hand for the new headquarters. The desirable plot seemed unattainable. But prayer was constantly being made about the whole matter, and God began to work.

One day the agent telephoned and said he thought the owners of the property might sell for $105,000. A sudden reduction of 65,000 Malay dollars! It was a most tempting offer, for the property was worth the price originally asked. Had there been $105,000 in the new buildings fund, no doubt the offer would have been accepted. But there was only $85,000 in the fund.

"We can give $85,000 for the property, and no more," said the Mission representative.

"I only have power of attorney for $90,000," replied the agent.

It was no use. There just was not that extra $5,000 in hand. The telephone receiver was replaced rather sadly.

To be so near obtaining that eminently suitable plot, so urgently needed, and then to lose it, just for lack of $5,000! But the matter was in God's hands, and the lack of $5,000 presented no problem to Him. In this case, He just brought the price down! The telephone bell rang less than five minutes after the receiver had been replaced.

"Take the thing!" said a rather irate voice at the other end of the wire. "Take it for $85,000!" And so the money that had been coming in, much of it contributed by members of the Mission whose own purses were by no means overfull, proved sufficient after all. It is worthy of note that the adjacent property had been sold for $2 per square foot, while the Mission property was obtained at the rate of $1 per square foot, and the seven bed-roomed house into the bargain!

What the Lord was able and willing to do in the provision of a place to live in in Singapore He has proved equally able and willing to do in the cities and villages and hamlets into which the forward movement workers went. Many of those forward movement workers were women. The entry into completely unevangelized areas was dependent on the obtaining of suitable accommodation, for native inns in the East are no places for women to live unprotected. How, for instance, could Miss Frances Williamson and Miss Marie Barham be encouraged to go to the remote island of Mindoro in the Philippines to start work amongst the neglected Mangyan tribes there, if they had nowhere to live? But God had a place prepared. An earnest Filipino Christian living on the coast at San Teodoro heard that missionaries wanted to come to preach to the Mangyan tribesmen. He was glad. He offered the missionaries a little home, free of charge. It was a shack on stilts, built for his newly-married daughter on the palm-fringed beach by his saw-mill. His daughter did not want to live there, so it was lying empty—God's provision for His servants. That shack was the Mission's first foothold in the island where there are now thirty-four C.I.M. missionaries, living in eleven different centres, and pressing further and further into the mountains and jungles to carry the news of a Saviour to the uttermost parts. It is perhaps true to say that they are going forward shack by shack, for in shacks they must live if they would become as the Mangyan to win the Mangyan. And none of the places the Lord has provided for His servants to inhabit in the East or the West has a more touching story than some of those shacks, built by wistful jungle dwellers for the "Amerikanos" who have come, wonder of all wonders, to live among "us poor Mangyan". One of them, a rickety shanty about twelve feet square, nevertheless commands a view that a millionaire might envy. High up on a wooded hillside overlooking the sparkling eastern sea, the site was specially chosen by the Mangyan who built it—"because we knew you like things beautiful", they explained shyly to their missionaries. When God's provision comes from such simple, loving hearts, who would remain unmoved at the sight of such a place to live in?

The homes of the people in Central Thailand are also mainly built on stilts, but they are much bigger, better finished, cleaner and stronger than those of the jungle dwellers of Mindoro. When it was decided that the thirteen unevangelized provinces in Central Thailand must be entered in the name of the Lord, and that the first entry should be made by one man and four women, again "places to live in" had to be found. To become as a Thai to gain the Thai, Thai houses were needed! But how to obtain them? The ex-China missionary deputed to find them, although a fluent speaker of Mandarin, was but a little child when it came to speaking Thai, and he certainly would not have thought of house-hunting in the manner a friendly missionary of the American Bible Society showed him! Mr. L. C. Wood wrote home describing those house-hunting excursions in 1952:

> To our great joy we have been able to open two mission stations in the central provinces during the last six weeks, one at Paknampho and the other at Saraburi. House-hunting in Thailand seems to require a special combination of tactful persistence and courteous audacity. I should have been completely at a loss as to how to go about this task but for the help of Mr. Peter Voth. He accompanied me on two trips of discovery, one by road and one by rail, for the first of which he kindly made his car available. We would tour the town until we came upon a house that seemed suitable from the point of view of location as well as size and general convenience, and then my friend would go in and fetch a conversational compass which would finally bring the owner of the house face to face with the startling proposition that he should move out in order that we, strangers, foreigners, and the propagators of a strange religion to boot, should move in! And the amazing thing is that these strange operations were just over 66 per cent. successful, for we got two out of the three houses that we angled for. So much for the human side of things; on the Divine side we are convinced that these houses were prepared for us of the Lord, and given to us in answer to prayer.

So we could continue. The very mundane task of house-hunting that superintendents in the various countries have had to undertake may not seem, on the face of it, very closely related to the spread of the Gospel—and yet, in actual fact, the spread of the Gospel depended on it! Early in 1956 seven people were baptized in Uthai in Central Thailand, where two young women missionaries had been living. Those seven people, and others who are also believing, would still be living in spiritual darkness had not a rather hot American stepped ashore from a tiny river launch one day, feeling somewhat overwhelmed at the prospect of looking for a house in this town in which he knew not one soul, and started walking up the main street giving out tracts. His knowledge of the Thai language was so limited that to attempt street preaching alone was out of the question! How negotiate for a house? Indeed, how *find* a house for rent? But as he walked on, a prayer in his heart, a well dressed young Thai cycling past dismounted and spoke courteously to him—in English. Through that contact, a house was found, and from that house souls are being found to become a habitation of God through the Spirit. Shall He who Himself seeks a home in human hearts deny a home to His servants to live in? Writes the superintendent of Central Thailand, "Though there is a real housing shortage here, not one of our workers has been greatly delayed by lack of accommodation when the decision has been made to open a centre."

One more story must suffice for this section. It had been decided that a centre for the distribution of Christian literature throughout the great Republic of Indonesia be opened in Djakarta, the capital. But where was the necessary property to be found? Here again, it seemed out of the question to obtain anything suitable at a moderate figure. But God was preparing for this need also, and He did it in a very remarkable way.

Late in 1955 a wealthy Chinese business man in Djakarta, had a dream. It was a very vivid dream, in which God told him to build a church! Now this man was not a Christian, but a Buddhist! Yet so deeply impressed was he by the dream that he was impelled to obey. He procured a plot of land, had a large assembly hall built with a little house at the back for the prospective pastor—and then started looking for some Christian group to whom he could give the assembly room and sell the little house!

It so happened that a Chinese Christian in the city heard about it. This man had received his Bible training from a C.I.M. missionary when still in China, and knowing that the Mission contemplated opening work in Djakarta, he got in touch with George Steed, superintendent of the work in Indonesia. It seemed almost too wonderful to be true, that this beautiful property could be made available, but made available it was. It is now in the possession of the Mission, the place where the Christian Witness Press in the Republic will have its centre, the missionaries their home, and a Chinese Christian group, the Ling Liang Tang, their Bible class room! The price paid for the whole property was about the equivalent of what would have been demanded for "key money" alone had it been rented in the ordinary way.

Away in Canada another property deal had taken place which provided the money required for the purchase of that Djakarta building, and much more besides. The Mission owned two large houses in Toronto, which years ago was the North American headquarters of C.I.M. Later, headquarters were moved to Philadelphia, and for that and other reasons the property in Toronto was now larger than was required. Early in 1954 it was suggested that one of the houses might be sold, but for some reason the Council eventually advised against doing so, and the property was retained. That decision, which was taken with no idea of what was to happen, brought the Mission thousands of dollars! A few months later building authorities reviewing the district came to the conclusion that it was eminently suitable for the erection of blocks of flats. The Mission property happened to adjoin a small park, so that site was particularly desirable. Overnight the property quadrupled in value! When the C.I.M. council met again a unanimous vote was passed that it should be sold! The deals were eventually put through, smaller and more suitable property obtained for the Mission centre and retired workers' home, and the sum of U.S.$125,000 forwarded to Singapore. It came at a time when remittances were low, and very heavy expenditure was looming up if the plans for advance were to be put into operation. Once more, tangible confirmation of God's will to go forward has been provided.

It is exactly ninety years ago, as these words are being penned, that the *Lammermuir* party, escorted by Hudson Taylor, was preparing to sail for China. Such a launching forth into the deep as the departure of that party of eighteen young men and women from the shores of England was perhaps unprecedented in the history of missions. They were going to the other side of the world, to enter a country fanatically opposed to Westerners in order to proclaim salvation through faith in an unknown God; a country in which they would have no means of earning a livelihood. Unlike the members of already existing missionary societies, however, they had no assurance of support from organizations in the homeland, at whose responsibility they went forth. They went because, with their young leader, they believed that if they did God's work in God's way, God would supply them with what they needed. They were prepared to put that confidence in God to the test, and as they did so they found it worked. God's work demanded their most strenuous efforts, physically, mentally and spiritually. God's way was an unobtrusive self-denying way, and often required that they be prepared to humble themselves, and endure with patience that which was contrary to the desires of nature. But as for matters of food and clothing and places to live in, the provision of these was not their anxiety. Their Master had made Himself responsible for them when He committed Himself in the utterance "Seek ye first the kingdom of God and His righteousness, and all these things shall be added unto you." That was their gilt-edged security, as it is ours to-day, and has remained unaffected by changing world conditions. The purpose of this book is to bear testimony to God's ability to provide, and His willingness to do so, all the material needs of those who trust Him. And even in those times when we are sadly conscious of personal failure and weakness of faith, the testimony remains unchanged, for

IF WE BELIEVE NOT, YET HE ABIDETH FAITHFUL:
HE CANNOT DENY HIMSELF.